TRUMP U.

TRUMP U.

THE INSIDE STORY OF TRUMP UNIVERSITY

STEPHEN GILPIN

OR Books
New York

Published by OR Books, New York
Visit our website at www.orbooks.com

First printing 2018

Cataloging-in-Publication data is available from the Library of Congress.

ISBN 978-1-94486-973-1 paperback
ISBN 978-1-94486-974-8 ebook

Text design by Under|Over. Typeset by AarkMany Media, Chennai, India.

Published for the book trade by OR Books in partnership with Counterpoint Press. Distributed to the trade by Publishers Group West.

One warm evening three years after the end of Trump University, I drove from my office on West Thirty-Sixth Street to the West Side Highway, then south to the Brooklyn Battery Tunnel, finally arriving at my home on Ocean Parkway in Brooklyn. My experience at Trump University was like a strange dream that was gradually fading. I had moved on with my life and was happy to be serving as the director of the New York Real Estate Institute. In the old days with Trump U., I had a car and driver, but now I drove myself, and I didn't mind. After parking in the underground garage of my apartment building and walking through the lobby, I glanced out to the street before I got into the elevator. I noticed a sheriff's car parked in front of the building with two officers standing next to it. Not thinking much about it, I went directly to my top floor penthouse. I was surprised to find a subpoena taped to my door. Shocked and rattled, I took the document and went inside.

Before I had a chance to open the envelope there was a knock. When I opened the door, my neighbor said breathlessly, "Steve, there were people here looking for you—police officers!"

Police? A subpoena? What was going on? My first thought was that I was being sued. I didn't know why the police were involved, but after I thanked my nosy neighbor and closed the door, I read the subpoena.

I was being subpoenaed to be a witness in the State of New York's lawsuit against Donald J. Trump and Trump University. Like everyone else, I had read in the newspaper that on August 24, 2013, Attorney General Eric Schneiderman had filed suit against Trump for fraud, alleging that Trump University was a scam built around the practice of upselling gullible people. The suit maintained that the sole purpose of the for-profit company was separating students from their money as quickly and efficiently as possible.

This lawsuit was serious business. *Any* lawsuit involving Donald J. Trump was serious business. The State of New York was a powerful opponent. As for Donald Trump, I knew that if you got in his way he'd flatten you like roadkill and then blame you for stepping in front of his armored midnight-blue Rolls-Royce.

As a former employee of Trump University, I was caught in the middle. I didn't want to be collateral damage in this titanic struggle. With a rising feeling of panic, I knew I had to hire a top lawyer. I also knew that I could not *afford* a top lawyer.

I called up what was left of the organization—by this time there was just a skeleton staff and an office. I spoke to an old colleague who was still there and explained my situation. He offered to connect me with a lawyer who worked for Trump U. I thought this was a generous offer. Mr. Trump had the back of his former employees. Little did I know that while one friendly hand was on my shoulder, the other held a sharp knife.

I called the lawyer. His name was Avi Schick. After listening to what I said, he told me without hesitation, "Stay quiet and stay in your house until we meet. Don't talk to anybody. Don't talk to the news."

News? What would the news want with me, Stephen Gilpin, a meat-and-potatoes real estate guy? I soon found out. I went to Starbucks to get coffee and found reporters stalking me and taking pictures of me, and soon the story appeared in the *New York Post*.

This was not what I wanted. While it may be Donald Trump's bedrock belief that the highest goal in life is to get your picture in the newspaper, it was not my style. I liked being anonymous. During my next phone call with Mr. Schick, he told me that I would need to meet with him for at least two hours every day to prepare for my deposition.

How on earth could I afford that? Schick was a heavyweight. He was one of those guys who charged thousands of dollars an hour just to talk to you on the phone. In fact, while he was representing Trump University at the moment, he had previously served as deputy attorney general in the office of the New York State Attorney General—the same folks who were now suing Trump—where he had represented the state in significant litigations, investigations, and appeals in both federal and state trial and appellate courts. He had led all aspects of the state's investigation and litigation involving executive compensation at the New York Stock Exchange, and he had also been the state's lead lawyer handling all litigation related to the $200 billion tobacco master settlement agreement.

And now Avi Schick was working for Trump *against* his former bosses. Go figure. I guess that was just part of the strange and wondrous world of lawyers.

Schick said not to worry about the cost. He said that Donald Trump would personally pay my legal fees. That sounded good, but would I also be getting paid for the time that I missed from work? "Oh no, you've got it wrong," Schick replied. "He's paying your legal fees. That's it."

"How am I supposed to meet with you for two hours every day?" I asked. "Is Donald Trump paying for me to stop working at my job?"

"No. What time do you get done with work?"

"Eight o'clock."

"Great," he said. "I'll stay later at the office and we'll do it at night." I told Schick I'd think about it.

After pouring myself a double bourbon on the rocks, I sat down and realized that I had a tough choice to make. As a Trump University insider, I was either going to testify for the state and give evidence *against* Trump University, or I was going to go with Donald Trump and *support* the university. Once, I had admired Donald Trump and thought the school could have been fixed. I also wasn't sure that the state's lawsuit was justified. To me, unhappy students—and there were many of them—should have been given refunds, but was it a criminal case?

I suppose I believed there had been a glimmer of purpose behind what we had been doing at Trump U, because it had been my job to attempt to deliver real knowledge and real value to the students. I had been the token real estate expert and lovable knucklehead among the many salespeople and motivational speakers aggressively selling the Trump message of boundless wealth. Aside from Donald Trump himself, for three years, I was just about the only guy in the organization who had substantial, down-to-earth real estate experience.

I talked to Schick again. He pressured me to go with Trump. "Trust me, son," he said. "You don't want the legal fees that you're going to have to pay if you go by yourself. You're better off going with me. I'll keep you clean. I'll keep you out of jail."

"Whoa," I said. "Jail? What the hell could I go to *jail* for?"

Being a witness was one thing, but how could I get incarcerated for this mess? It was not my responsibility. I was a W-2 employee. I didn't start the company. I didn't manage it. I was paid by Trump University. The company had gone under, but not by my hand. If there was criminality, it wasn't from me. I had been trying to *help* the students.

But Schick made it sound like the employees might be going to jail if we didn't play ball and defend Trump University. Of course, now I know that Schick was selling me a story. When you're a W-2 employee, your only responsibility is to do what your boss tells you to do. You don't make policy. But Schick sold me this story the same way Trump sells his steaks or his golf courses or any other products. The exact truth doesn't matter as much as the **emotional impact**. Trump knows how to play to his target's fears and desires. My fear—like any rational person—was of getting ground up like hamburger between the massive legal machines operated by the state of New York and by Donald Trump. When you're on a battlefield and you see the tanks rumbling in from both directions, you'd better choose sides or get the hell out of the way.

I was never a target of any lawsuit or criminal complaint. But at that moment, with the subpoena from the State of New York in my hand, what Schick and others in the Trump Organization told me was very convincing. They said that I couldn't go against Trump.

They said I would get crushed. They said that if I stuck with Trump, he would back me and make sure I was clear of all liability. They always made it sound like the employees would be in trouble. If we were on our own, we would not have Donald Trump to back us, and we would get in big legal trouble and would have to pay legal fees for years and years to come.

They insisted that we should use their lawyers. And why not? They were good lawyers, and Donald Trump would pay them.

I still had a choice to make. I considered becoming a witness for the state, but the New York Attorney General's office played rough with me. They scared the shit out of me and attacked me when they could have persuaded me. They made going with Trump an easy decision. Perhaps Schick was right. In my mind, it was just possible that I might be a target, too.

I decided to cast my fate with my old bosses at Trump University and work with Avi Schick. He said, "Good. You've made the right choice. We'll start work tonight. Be at my office at eight-thirty."

As I walked to Avi Schick's office for my first prep session, I thought to myself, *how did I get here?* It seemed bizarre and frightening. Just a day earlier, I thought the Trump University nightmare was behind me and my life was now going to be smooth sailing. But instead I was fighting for my life—again.

I hoped that my own wits and capacity for survival would get me through the ordeal. I also believed I had the truth on my side. I should have known better. At Trump University, "truth" was a relative concept, subject to revision on a whim. Even so, I believed that the truth would have more authority in court. But how did I get here? What had been the long and winding path to this moment?

1.

In 1990, I enrolled in Luzerne County Community College in Nanticoke, a town a few miles south of Wilkes-Barre, Pennsylvania. Then I went to King's College in Wilkes-Barre, a small Catholic school founded in 1946 by the Congregation of Holy Cross from the University of Notre Dame. While in school, I did male modeling, starting off walking a runway at fashion shows in Pennsylvania. Soon I was earning enough to become independent.

One day I received a call from an agent, and the next thing I knew I was in New York City for a shoot. It was a huge rush, and I wanted to keep doing it. I got more work in the city. I'd go there every weekend after my week at school. I modeled for Levi Strauss and other clothing companies. I modeled the Michael Jackson Elizabeth Taylor tribute jacket for men. Photographers ran the modeling world, and they introduced me to other photographers, who put me in their books. Soon I was getting calls without even auditioning.

Through modeling, I met a community of partiers who flocked to underground clubs. Some of my new friends were glamorous, some were wealthy, and some were both. They came together for the parties, which would always turn into all-nighters. The rich and famous came to these parties, too. Once I saw Eartha Kitt, who played Catwoman in the original Batman TV series, posing on a motorcycle, stark-ass naked.

While I was in New York, I stayed at the Gramercy Park Hotel. Built in 1925, the venerable Renaissance revival landmark had been home to luminaries like Humphrey Bogart (who married his first wife Helen Menken there), the Joseph P. Kennedy family (including young John F. Kennedy), Babe Ruth (a regular bar patron), and James Cagney and his wife.

Later decades saw people like Bob Marley and Bob Dylan, actor Matt Dillon, playwright David Mamet, the English punk band the Clash, Madonna, Debbie Harry, and David Bowie. I liked the vibe of New York energy and wealth. It was a long way from sleepy Pittston, Pennsylvania.

One night, a modeling friend and I went to a party in an abandoned subway tunnel. These were illegal gatherings that promoters would stage deep beneath New York's streets. We gathered at midnight on a certain block, where we had been instructed to approach a designated "agent." Having checked our names against the list, the agent told us to join a group of other people who were walking down a seemingly deserted street. Suddenly the people started disappearing! When we got closer, we saw that our fellow revelers were dropping down into an open manhole. When my turn came, I took a deep breath, prayed that I wasn't making a horrible life-altering mistake, and climbed down the long ladder. After negotiating a dank corridor and descending a set of iron stairs, I found myself in a huge graffiti-covered concrete chamber lit by candles and flashlights. A motley marching band (there was no electricity down there for electric instruments) blared raucous tunes from a platform. It was like a bizarre scene from a post-apocalyptic movie.

As a denizen of New York nightlife, I popped Quaaludes, got high, and drank with friends. There were no limits. We seemed to be invincible. It got so bad that I was taking drugs to wake up in the morning and taking drugs to put me to sleep at night. The lifestyle was incredibly seductive. I experienced a life that had no consequences and one that proved that even too much was never enough. *It's scary, but I'm cool,* I told myself. *I can do it.*

Fortunately, a friend took me aside. One night in the wee hours of the morning after a party, we went out to a pizza shop in Greenwich Village for a slice. My friend was a famous photographer who worked for Robert Mapplethorpe, whom I had met through my modeling. He was successful and had connections. He was a photographer for all the major magazines as well as for retailers like Abercrombie and Fitch. He was also doing his own work. He and other photographer friends, including Gene Pappis and the Morris brothers, saw me for what I was—a naïve kid who should not have been hanging out with these wild people on weekends. They were worried about my being caught up into that lifestyle. My friend told me that I would be eaten alive in New York City, that I would never survive, that I would be used, abused, and tossed aside like a half-eaten cheeseburger. He saw that I had potential, but he insisted that instead of partying I needed to start paying attention to the business. It was advice that I tried to take to heart. Maybe it kept me from doing anything *really* stupid.

As a model, I was often sent by my agency to mingle at private parties from Boston to Florida. My job was to stand around looking handsome. (Can you believe it? Getting paid just to stand around at a party?) At these events I didn't have much to do but contemplate the lifestyle of the one percent. Perhaps because of my experience helping my uncle at his house and renovating other family properties, I started looking at the homes in which I was loitering. In retrospect, I suppose this was because the houses were more interesting to me than the boring rich people who owned them. I asked myself, *what turns a house into a mansion?* It was then that I first became interested in real estate, which would eventually become my life's calling.

While I was figuring out what to do with my life, the man whose path I would soon cross had already built a real estate empire and was embarking on even bigger plans. In the early 1970s, Donald J. Trump had started his career in Brooklyn with his developer father, Fred Trump. Most people know the basic story about Fred and Donald Trump, but Donald's penchant for making money can be traced back to his paternal grandmother, Elizabeth Christ Trump.

She was born in Germany on October 10, 1880. When she was twenty-two years old she married Friedrich Trump, a thirty-three-year-old entrepreneur who had been to America and had been successful in various businesses. The newlyweds moved to New York City, where Friedrich found work as a barber and also as the manager of a restaurant and hotel. He and Elizabeth lived at 1006 Westchester Avenue in the German-speaking Morrisania neighborhood of the Bronx. In 1904, their first child, a daughter, was born.

Despite living in a German neighborhood, Elizabeth was thoroughly homesick. For this reason, Friedrich decided to move the family back to Germany. He sold his assets in America, and before Christmas they were living in Kallstadt, a village near Mannheim in Rhineland-Palatinate. But Friedrich had military draft problems. The family had barely arrived in Germany when, on December 24, 1904, the Department of the Interior in Germany announced an investigation to deport Trump from the country. Officially, they found that he had violated the Resolution of the Royal Ministry of the Interior number 9916, an 1886 law that stripped German citizenship from any man who emigrated to North America to avoid military service. A year later, after an unsuccessful appeal in which Friedrich announced, "We are loyal Germans and stand behind the high Kaiser and the mighty German Reich," the family was expelled and forced to make the journey back to the United States.

In 1905, their second child Frederick Christ Trump (who was called Fred) was born, and they set up house on 177th Street in the Bronx. After Elizabeth gave birth to her third child, John, the family moved to Queens, where Friedrich began to develop real estate. In May 1918, Friedrich, with his thick mustache and bushy eyebrows, and young Fred, with his blond parted hair, were walking along the German shops of Jamaica Avenue when Friedrich said he felt ill.

"Then, he died," Fred Trump recounted to author Gwenda Blair for a Trump family biography. "Just like that."

His sudden death was not unusual. Known as "Spanish Flu" or "La Grippe," the influenza pandemic of 1918-1919 was a global nightmare. With total deaths somewhere between twenty and forty million people, influenza killed more people than World War I. It has been called the most devastating epidemic in recorded world history. To those infected, death came with shocking swiftness and savagery. Victims were struck with illness on the street and died before reaching home. One physician wrote that patients with seemingly ordinary influenza would rapidly "develop the most vicious type of pneumonia that has ever been seen," and when cyanosis—bluish skin—appeared in the patients, it was "simply a struggle for air until they suffocate." The physicians of the time were helpless against this indiscriminate killer.

But Friedrich Trump had been busy in the New World: he left his young family an estate valued at $31,359—about half a million dollars today. Rather than being paralyzed with grief, Elizabeth Trump swung into action. While raising her three children, she took over the management of her husband's properties. Showing a remarkable talent for keeping the real estate business going, she hired a contractor to build houses on an empty piece of property left by her husband. She sold the houses on the property, and then lived off the mortgages paid by the new owners. She groomed her three children to continue the family business after they had each finished school, but young Fred wanted to start earlier, so she founded a real estate company and called it Elizabeth Trump & Son. Since Fred was only eighteen years old, she had to perform the real estate closings for him and sign all legal documents on his behalf.

Fred turned twenty-two in 1927, and that was when Elizabeth Trump & Son was formally incorporated. While Fred became quite successful, his mother Elizabeth still remained involved in the business throughout her life. Even in her seventies, she would collect coins from the laundromats in Trump buildings. She died on June 6, 1966, at the age of eighty-five.

At age twenty-eight, Fred won the mortgage service business of a troubled German bank, and by 1938 was bragging in the papers about the "throngs visiting" his developments in Brooklyn. That year, the *Brooklyn Daily Eagle* referred to him first as a prominent Long Island builder, then as the "Henry Ford of the home-building industry."

His ego grew with the press, and Fred became a showman. On a sweltering day in July 1939, New Yorkers seeking sun and surf at Coney Island were astonished to see a yacht, sixty-five-feet long, outfitted with enormous Trump signs and loudspeakers that blasted recordings of "The Star-Spangled Banner" and "God Bless America." The Trump Show Boat was hard to miss. As the boat floated toward the beach, the crew released brightly-colored sword-fish-shaped balloons, each of which was redeemable for $25 in cash or $250 toward a new Trump Home. Bathers stampeded to snatch them up.

Fred was more than willing to adjust the facts to fit current reality—just as his son Donald would later do. During the Second World War, anti-German sentiment was strong. Fears of sabotage led to laws barring people of German descent from boarding boats and even from entering some cities. Perhaps to avoid problems in selling properties to Jewish customers, Fred Trump began to present himself and his family as descendants of immigrants from Sweden. This became the standard family line, even long after the war ended. Even Donald Trump, not known to be shy about embellishing facts, eventually questioned the need for this dissimulation. According to his cousin John Walter, the Trump family historian, when Trump was planning his best seller *The Art of the Deal* in the mid-1980s, he asked his father, "Do I have to do this Swedish thing?" I suppose the answer was "yes," because in the book, published in 1987, he asserted that his father's story was "classic Horatio Alger," and that his grandfather Friedrich "came here from Sweden as a child."

In 1936, Fred Trump married Mary MacLeod, who had been born in Scotland. They settled together in Queens. Beginning with Fred "Freddy" Trump Jr., born in 1938, they had five children. Donald, the fourth child, was born on June 14, 1946 in Jamaica Estates, Queens. Of his four siblings, three are still alive: Maryanne, Elizabeth, and Robert. Freddy, who as a youth was the heir apparent to the family business, eventually died in 1981 from alcoholism.

Years later, Donald Trump told the Christian Broadcasting Network that Freddy "had everything going, but when he went to college for some reason he started drinking. That was before the drug age and before the other things . . . but he drank and he drank a lot and he started drinking more and more and he ultimately died of alcoholism." As a result, Trump said, "I never drank." He called it a "defining moment."

While attending the Wharton School at the University of Pennsylvania, Donald worked for Elizabeth Trump & Son, and in 1968 he officially joined the company. When Freddy left the family business to pursue a career as a pilot (and eventually his self-destruction through alcohol), the path opened up for Donald Trump to inherit the Trump empire. He was given control of the company in 1971, and in one of his first acts, he renamed it the Trump Organization—the name it holds today.

Fred Sr. passed away in 1999, triggering a nasty familial fight over his will. When he died, Fred Sr. left an estate with an estimated worth of $100-300 million. His will divided most of his estate between the families of his surviving children, leaving a pittance to the widow and children of Freddy, Donald's deceased older brother.

Freddy had a son named Fred III, who in turn had a son named William Trump. As a baby, William had been diagnosed with infantile spasms, a rare disorder that led to cerebral palsy. This chronic illness required a lifetime of 24-hour nursing care and frequent visits to medical specialists and emergency rooms. Fortunately for the baby and his family, William was covered under a medical plan that was paid for by a Trump family company.

In March of 2000, Fred III and his wife Lisa filed suit in Queens Surrogate's Court, claiming that Fred Sr. had been suffering from Alzheimer's disease and that his will had been "procured by fraud and undue influence" on the part of Donald, his brother Robert, a New York businessman, and his sister Maryanne, a federal judge in Newark, New Jersey. Fred III and Lisa demanded a larger cut of the estate.

The response was swift. On March 30th, Fred III received a certified letter telling him that the medical benefits provided to his family by The Trump Organization would end on May 1st. The letter prompted Fred III to return to court, this time in Nassau County, where a judge ordered the Trumps to restore the health coverage until the dispute was resolved. "I will stick to my guns," Fred III told Heidi Evans, a reporter for the *Daily News*. "I just think it was wrong. These are not warm and fuzzy people. They never even came to see

William in the hospital. Our family puts the 'fun' in dysfunctional."
Fred III's sister Mary told the *Daily News*, "William is my father's
grandson. He is as much a part of that family as anybody else. He
desperately needs extra care."

Donald Trump, for his part, was unapologetic about his
actions. "Why should we give him medical coverage?" he told the
Daily News. When the reporter asked him if he thought he might
appear cold-hearted given the baby's medical condition, he replied,
"I can't help that. It's cold when someone sues my father. Had he
come to see me, things could very possibly have been much different for them." Donald Trump has since said the suit was settled
"amicably."

Having established himself in Brooklyn, Donald crossed the
river into Manhattan, where he opened his signature landmark
Trump Tower in 1983. Looming fifty-eight stories over Fifth Avenue,
it was an impressive sight. Originally the tallest all-glass structure
in Manhattan, its pampered residents enjoyed unobstructed views
of Central Park and midtown Manhattan and the status of the big
TRUMP name across the entrance.

One day when I was in New York and strolling along Fifth
Avenue, I wandered into the tower's gleaming lobby, covered in its
signature expensive pink white-veined marble. I saw the four gold-
painted elevators that transported visitors from the lobby to higher
floors. Someone said that one elevator led directly to the penthouse
where the Trump family lived in gilded splendor. I made my way
into the majestic five-level atrium, bedecked in rosy and yellow
marble and crowned with its skylight. I admired the sixty-foot-high
waterfall, with the suspended walkway providing breathtaking

views, while shops, cafés, and a pedestrian bridge crossed over the waterfall's sparkling pool.

What an impressive place! I could feel the power and smell the money. All around me were busy important people engaged in busy important things. The rousing song by the band Queen came into my head: "We are the champions! No time for losers, 'cause we are the champions!" Here within the opulent walls of Trump Tower there were no losers, only champions. Here, greed was not merely "good," as Gordon Gekko had said in the film *Wall Street*; it was celebrated as the highest calling of every citizen. If you weren't greedy, there was something wrong with you, and you deserved to live in your crummy apartment in the Bronx or your plain split-level ranch-style house in Pittston.

I was a kid working as a male model trying to break into the real estate business, standing inside one of the majestic creations of New York's most flamboyant wheeler-dealer, the biggest cultural personality since P.T. Barnum. Trump's book *The Art of the Deal* had been a best seller (of course, years later we learned that Trump hadn't penned a single word), and he seemed to live a charmed life. Even his disasters had the aura of greatness. Just 120 miles to the south, Trump had tried to expand and monopolize the casino industry in Atlantic City. After launching two casino complexes, Trump Castle and Trump Plaza, he acquired the unfinished palace-themed Taj Mahal Casino in 1988. He sunk over $1 billion into the project, making it the most expensive casino ever built at the time, as well as the tallest building in New Jersey.

"It's truly going to be an incredible place," he told reporters. "We're calling it the eighth wonder of the world."

Less than two weeks before this grandiose monument to Trump's ego opened, Marvin B. Roffman, a casino analyst at the Philadelphia-based investment firm Janney Montgomery Scott, told the *Wall Street Journal* that the Taj would need to reap $1.3 million a day just to make its interest payments, a sum no casino had ever achieved. In response, Trump demanded that Roffman be fired, and he threatened to sue the paper for libel.

However, Roffman was right. The Taj Mahal, choking on debt, was a disaster, and the bloated corpse quickly fell into the dark grave of Chapter 11 bankruptcy. It was soon followed by both Trump Plaza and Trump Castle. In an August 1990 report, New Jersey regulators noted the "sheer volume of debt" on Trump's holdings, and regulators warned that "the possibility of a complete financial collapse of the Trump Organization was not out of the question."

But Donald Trump worked his magic with the ledger books and juggled more debt. He consolidated his casinos into Trump Hotels & Casino Resorts, a publicly traded company. On June 14, 1996, he celebrated his fiftieth birthday at the Taj Mahal, serenaded by the angelic voices of the Beach Boys. A flurry of news articles heralded his triumphant return.

That same year he opened Trump's World's Fair, a fourth casino adjacent to Trump Plaza. It closed in 1999. In 2004, Trump Hotels & Casino Resorts filed for Chapter 11. The name of the company was changed to Trump Entertainment Resorts. Five years later, Trump Entertainment Resorts filed for Chapter 11. Trump resigned as chairman. In 2014, Trump Entertainment Resorts, a company with which Trump was no longer personally involved, filed for Chapter

11. Trump Plaza closed in September. The Taj Mahal reached a deal to stay open under the control of billionaire Carl Icahn.

On September 2, 2016, Carl Icahn's management team petitioned the state gambling regulators for permission to shut down the Trump Taj Mahal casino in October. The petition asked the New Jersey Division of Gaming Enforcement for permission to close the casino and to approve plans to wind down the table games, disconnect the slot machines, store the unused liquor, and destroy the cards, dice, and gambling chips. The petition claimed the casino was losing millions of dollars a month while the city's main casino workers union carried out a strike against it. Many strikers questioned whether Icahn truly planned to close it or whether the shutdown threat was a bluff to get the striking union to accept the casino's final offer.

Closing the Trump Taj Mahal would mean that for the first time since 1984, there would be no gaming emporium in Atlantic City bearing the Trump name. But for Donald Trump, every cloud had a golden lining, and the collapse of his gambling empire in New Jersey brought him a singular and breathtaking personal benefit. On October 1, 2016, the *New York Times* reported that as a result of the financial hemorrhaging of his casino business, Trump had declared a loss of $916 million on his 1995 income tax returns. It was a deduction so substantial it could have legally erased more than fifty million dollars a year in taxable income for the next eighteen years—or until 2013. The provision, known as net operating loss (NOL), allowed a generous array of deductions, business expenses, real estate depreciation, losses from the sale of business assets, and even operating losses to flow from the balance sheets of those partnerships, limited liability companies, and S corporations onto

Trump's personal tax returns. For example, the $916 million loss could have eliminated any federal income taxes Trump otherwise would have owed on the money he was paid for each episode of *The Apprentice*, or the roughly $45 million he was paid between 1995 and 2009 when he was chairman or chief executive of the publicly traded company he created to assume ownership of his doomed Atlantic City gambling palaces.

The pain of Trump's disastrous casino venture was further assuaged by a sweet deal from his buddy Chris Christie. When Christie became governor of New Jersey in 2002, the state's auditors and lawyers had been fighting for years to collect $30 million in overdue taxes owed by Trump's casinos. But soon after Christie took office, the state began to seek a settlement. In December 2011, after six years in court, the state agreed to accept just five million dollars—roughly seventeen cents on the dollar of what auditors said that the casinos owed.

Such are the rollercoaster fortunes of the unsinkable Donald Trump. Others may lose their fortunes at the gambling table of life, but somehow Trump managed to get all the chips on the table piled in front of him.

2.

So how did an ex-model end up at 40 Wall Street? In 1998, I started at Bank One Mortgage in Indianapolis as a desktop underwriter, processing loan applications. I also took classes at night. I looked up to the loan officers, who seemed to know everything. Then one day I realized that all they were really doing was taking applications and connecting people. I thought, *I can do that!*

A friend who was an attorney and a builder told me about a little-known technique for connecting buyers with homes for sale. The trick was to connect buyers with construction companies before any building even began. My friend, who came from a very wealthy banking family and who also ran a construction company, was the first person to understand my vision for connecting people and how to implement it in the Indianapolis area.

It was a simple system. First, the builder would create a "spec home"—a house built to specifications that was meant as a show-case property. No one would live in it. In fact, the builders would typically use it as an office. When a buyer wanted to build a new home, an appraiser would gauge the value of their proposed home by inspecting the existing spec home. By coordinating with the builder, the buyer could get a mortgage based on their home's value after it had been built. It was one-stop shopping and I wanted to organize it all. I was the young kid who was applying this new idea in the Indianapolis suburbs.

I knew people in real estate from my modeling days who could open doors for me: builders, developers, contractors, and construction people. The day I had the epiphany that I could do anything that loan officers could do, I quit my job and opened up a competitive mortgage company across the street. At the age of twenty, I became known as "The Mortgage Boy."

I knew the basic terminology of a mortgage and became known for educating the wealthy people in my modeling circles. I got together with my friends, and we started putting together a team: home inspectors, appraisers, and construction companies. When you came in to do a cash-out refinance, we used our own home inspector and our own mortgage broker. We had no middleman, so we could offer the lowest rates.

Then we added a financial consulting service. I asked the client, "So what are you going to do with this cash?" They could get rid of debt, but I also knew a lot about buying property, and the market was rising quickly. So we convinced customers to use that money to buy another property for residual income as an investment property. We still do this today.

Because it was important for me to get to know a network of people who could be investors, attending parties was a useful strategy to get my idea off the ground. One VIP party at the Indianapolis 500 that I wanted to attend was being held at the raceway in a tent. I didn't have an invitation, so I snuck in behind a group of people who had their badges hanging around their necks. I was quickly confronted by a security guard who demanded to see my VIP pass. He was ready to throw me out when, miraculously, a stranger stepped forward and vouched for me. It turned out he had seen my mortgage advertisements in an Indianapolis newspaper. He told the security guard, "Don't worry about it. He's with me." We hung out and became friends. He had a lot of influential stockbroker friends. He was the first person to fund me. He gave me fifteen thousand dollars so I could open an office in Boston.

I continued to attend networking events and spoke with everyone I could about real estate, finance, mortgages, and my new approach. Eventually, I moved to Boston and brought in some new friends to fund a new venture. In Boston, I wasn't doing construction anymore. I wasn't working with buildings. I was working with homeowners and the equity in their houses. We brought in money hand over fist.

The people at my new venture were young, and we were all close friends. I had an idea, and for me to make money, I needed them all in. So I needed to show them that we would all make money. That's when I started to run my own themed parties. Now I was running the show.

At the same time, I tried returning to New York City, but the male modeling industry had changed. Racy underwear ads like the ones created by Calvin Klein were all the rage, and instead of modeling being based on your face and your body structure, it was now about how good you looked in your briefs. In the spring of 2001, I tried out for the Abercrombie & Fitch periodical *A&F Quarterly*. The model who got the job would be in the issue featuring Kyle and Lane

Carlson, twin brothers with muscular bodies who worked for Elite, a large modeling agency. They became famous for a nude shoot they did with the photographer Bruce Weber, and although they were both straight, they became icons in the gay community. For my audition, I also had to strip down naked. They were looking for a guy with perfect six-pack abs. Unfortunately, I had a mere four-pack, so I was out.

I had parties at my condo at 3 Appleton Street in Boston's historic South End. One blowout was attended by a journalist from New York who had contacted me because his magazine was doing a story about models who had successfully transitioned out of their modeling careers into something else, models who didn't end up as junkies lying in the gutter. I guess you could call it an inspirational piece. During the party, I had to go outside for a moment, and when I got back, I found the guy in my dining room shooting up.

On Friday morning, September 11, 2001, my friend Rob shook me awake. Normally I would have been snug in my own bed on Appleton Street, but I was hungover from the previous night, and I found myself lying on his sofa in his apartment on the sixth floor of the luxurious Tremont on the Common. "Wake up, man," he kept telling me. The World Trade Center was burning. We sat there like everyone else that day, glued to the news.

That afternoon, there was a loud knock at the door, and I opened it to find an FBI agent in the corridor. He said they needed to inspect our apartment for fugitives. I later learned that one of the 9/11 terrorists had stayed in the building and had left early that morning. A woman associated with the fugitives had also fled. She just packed her bags and abandoned the place. The entire building was on lockdown as the FBI investigated.

The terrorist attack on the World Trade Center triggered a financial panic, and investors who were refinancing their houses and buying investment properties suddenly wanted to pull out. I lost sixteen clients that week, and my mortgage business went down the drain.

During this time, I knew I needed to do something to reinvent myself. I knew I was partying too much. But I didn't know how to stop. Surprisingly, my mother had the answer. For my entire life, my controlling, self-serving mother had only looked out for herself. But I had made so much money in Boston, and had sent so much money to her, that she now considered me to be her cash cow. If I had a problem that impacted my ability to earn money, it was now *her* problem. She needed me to earn. If I needed to refinance and start fresh, somewhere away from the crash in New York City, she could help with that, too. To help herself, she helped me.

On a cold, clear morning in October, she loaded up my station wagon with luggage and our Corgis, and we drove straight to our family friends Debbie and Glenn's house in Kissimmee, Florida.

In the nineteenth century, Kissimmee had been a busy little city with vibrant citrus groves, but two consecutive freezes in 1894 and 1895 wiped out the industry. The local economy then shifted to cattle raising. This lasted until 1971, when Walt Disney World opened in nearby Lake Buena Vista. As the Orlando area became what's now called the "Theme Park Capital of the World," tourism and development supplanted cattle ranching. Today, most folks in Kissimmee work either for Walt Disney or Wal-Mart. In the panic following 9/11, swampy central Florida was considered a safe haven. Nobody wanted to bomb Florida. Even better, the housing market there had not been dampened as badly as in Boston and New York.

Staying with Debbie and Glenn was like being in a private rehab facility. I lived on a horse farm in a mansion with seven bedrooms, four bathrooms, a big living room, a dining room, a study, a library, and a three-car garage. Lots of snakes lurked in the grassy fields. I wasn't allowed any money, alcohol, or a phone. I had to ask for and pay a quarter every time I wanted a cigarette. I wasn't allowed to leave. I was a willing prisoner, because I knew that I needed the help. It was an intervention to which I fully consented.

After three months, I was able to return to what I did well. So I started a new mortgage business. This time, I wasn't allowed to touch the money. Debbie and Glenn acted like guardians without having actual power of attorney. It was a family business. Debbie and Glenn supplied starting funds and acted as my parents. My mother, who had driven me to Florida and then turned around and gone home, was cut off as a bad influence in my life.

I reconstituted my real estate company in Florida and rode the Bush-era real estate boom to the top. I developed the investment philosophy that, in addition to making money, you can do good things in a community. I invented the bus tour model of teaching real estate, where students ride a bus into the field to inspect and consider real properties. I found great joy in inspiring and educating those wanting to follow the American dream of owning property. I acted as an advisor and mentor, and I also wrote articles for magazines and websites.

I told all my clients to refinance their houses as investment properties to get residual income. I was such a deal maker! Some of my clients broke down in tears when they became property owners, and many are still friends of mine today. It was honest and pure. I felt like I was changing the world for the better.

I was buying properties and doing a few flips myself. I had my mortgages team, my appraisal company, and my home inspection company. I was back. I felt on top of the world. By 2004, my real estate company had grown to 3,000 realtors.

I invested in building communities, not simply for profit but for the greater good of a neighborhood. I also threw wild parties, but this time I only served alcohol, not drugs. My drink of choice was whiskey, but I kept my self-destructive tendencies in check.

I named one event "Midsummer Night's Dream," and it was held in the house and garage of one of my investment properties. Along each side of the driveway leading to the garage, we installed a steel trench fueled with propane gas. When the gas was lit, the arriving guests walked safely through a corridor of waist-high flames to enter the party. As an added festive touch, I had acrobats on stilts flipping and jumping through the fire on both sides.

As the guests entered the house, an actress dressed as Marilyn Monroe opened curtains to let the guests into a blue iridescent room filled with white butterflies. As they walked through the house, each room was a completely different color.

Events such as this were not unique to me. My excesses mirrored the excesses of the Florida real estate industry at that time. All around me, houses were selling as fast as builders could slap them together. The most pathetic tear-downs were being bought and flipped for huge profits.

New houses were getting bigger, too; this was the era of the McMansions, those enormous boxes with soaring twenty-foot ceilings and vast open spaces in which an entire village could live.

The garages of these houses were like huge warehouses for the big SUVs, motorcycles, jet skis, boats, and lawn tractors that every middle-class family had to have. With bigger houses and higher demand came skyrocketing prices. Everyone wanted a house or a condo in Florida, and developers couldn't drain the mosquito-infested swamps and get rid of the alligators fast enough. Investors drove up the prices in a wild feeding frenzy of speculation. Banks were handing out jumbo mortgages to anyone who could hold a pen and sign their name. Everyone was making money in real estate.

More and more properties were being converted to rentals. The number of delinquent mortgages was inching up. I noticed that appraisals were going down. Houses that had been appraised at three hundred thousand in 2005 were now being appraised at two seventy-five, not three fifty.

I had bought a "Disney house" in Winter Park for $250,000. Built in 1955, it needed work, so I spruced it up, and it was appraised for $350,000. Then I went to Wells Fargo for a refinancing. I got the deal much too easily. The mortgage officer didn't verify my income or my assets. It was the very definition of predatory lending.

The Economist had written in July 2005, "Prices are being driven by speculative demand . . . . Investors are prepared to buy houses they will rent out at a loss, just because they think prices will keep rising—the very definition of a financial bubble. In the hope of a large gain, 'flippers' buy and sell new properties even before they are built. In Miami, as many as half of the original buyers resell new apartments in this way. Many properties change hands two or three times before somebody finally moves in."

A May 2006 *Fortune* magazine article on the U.S. housing bubble stated, "The great housing bubble has finally started to deflate. . . . In many once-sizzling markets around the country, accounts of dropping list prices have replaced tales of waiting lists for unbuilt condos and bidding wars over humdrum three-bedroom colonials."

As 2006 came to a close, I sensed I was about to lose everything. The housing market had peaked and began to slide. In March 2007, national home sales and prices both fell dramatically in the steepest plunge since the 1989 savings and loan crisis. The subprime mortgage industry collapsed due to soaring home foreclosure rates. It was all downhill from there.

This volatile market was an opportunity for people like Donald Trump. In *How to Build a Fortune*, his 2006 audiobook from Trump University, he answered a question about "gloomy predictions that the real estate market is heading for a spectacular crash," by saying, "I sort of hope that happens because then people like me would go in and buy." Trump was speaking with Jon Ward, a marketing consultant who "masterminded all the initial education programs for Trump University," according to his website.

"If there is a bubble burst, as they call it," continued Trump, "you know you can make a lot of money. If you're in a good cash position—which I'm in a good cash position today—then people like me would go in and buy like crazy."

On March 20, 2007 he told *The Globe and Mail,* "People have been talking about the end of the cycle for twelve years, and I'm excited if it is. I've always made more money in bad markets than in good markets." He advised investors that there were great deals in buying subprime mortgages at a discount and repossessed houses at low prices. Of course, Trump's properties wouldn't be affected by a real estate collapse. "I don't see the subprime problems affecting the higher-end stuff," he said.

A year later, when the housing crisis had spread like cancer across America, Trump University sent out sales pitches encouraging recipients to profit from the recession. An email to prospects in the Phoenix area—which was especially hard hit with rampant foreclosures—said, "This one class, how to profit from foreclosures, will get you started on the clearest, sure-fire, money-making opportunity available in a long, long time."

"Thousands of properties are available for pennies on the dollar," read another email bearing Trump's signature. "In today's down market I'm telling people to buy, buy, buy. Banks are selling foreclosed properties at pennies on the dollar."

3.

I knew that my Florida business didn't have much time left. The housing meltdown was coming, and everyone felt it but nobody knew what to do about it. The indicators were all there.

Although I ran a successful business with 3,000 real estate agents, I had no choice but to jump ship or I was going to go bankrupt. I didn't have a plan for where I was going to land—I just knew it would be somewhere in the Northeast. But I couldn't return to Boston, because even though I still had rental property there, when I had left after 9/11, I had left my team, who felt I had abandoned them. I can't say that I blamed them. On a whim, in December of 2006, I visited Universal Studios and submitted an application to join *The Apprentice*, the reality show starring Donald Trump.

The Apprentice had burst onto the nation's television screens during the winter and the spring of 2004. Produced and created by Mark Burnett, the premise of the show was the "ultimate job interview" in the "ultimate jungle" of New York, a job talent search for a person to head one of Trump's many companies. The meteoric popularity of the show led to Trump becoming known for his catchphrase, "You're fired!"

I figured that with my background, I could easily emerge victorious in the various tasks that the show demanded. Sell lemonade? Peddle stuff at a flea market? Create a sexy ad campaign? No problem.

After interviewing me at Universal, the casting people declined to offer me a spot on the show. Oh, well—I was not destined to become a reality TV star like Bill Rancic, the winner of season one, or Omarosa Manigault-Stallworth, who became everyone's favorite TV villain. Having dispensed with the crazy dream of becoming a household name, I went back to trying to figure out how I was going to sidestep the coming meltdown and reinvent my career.

A few months after my *Apprentice* interview I received a phone call from a woman who said she represented the Trump Organization. She had a very British accent and her voice was beautiful. She invited me to come in for an interview. She didn't tell me what the job was, just that they wanted to talk to me. It sounded too good and too far-fetched to be true. Just at the point where everything I had built was going to collapse, one of the richest real estate moguls in New York was offering me a safe haven? I thought my friends were pranking me. So I hung up on her.

But it was real. She called back. Her name was Sandra, and she asked me to come to New York. Since I frequently traveled to New York anyway, I was happy to oblige her on my own dime. I thought that because I was an actual real estate expert, this could be my meal ticket, the next step for my career. Back in those days, Donald Trump was not yet a political figure, but he was a big celebrity. Even my parents knew that you had to really be somebody to work for Donald Trump. And perhaps I wasn't meant to be a television star—perhaps fate had decided that my talents lay in real estate. In that case, working for Trump might be a very good match.

On a cold February morning, I got out of a cab at 40 Wall Street in New York: the Trump Building, where the Trump University offices were based. It was a grand old Art Deco landmark, built in 1928 as the Bank of Manhattan Building. It was the tallest building in the world until it was surpassed by the Chrysler Building in 1930. Both of them were soon outdone by the Empire State Building in 1931, which reigned as the world's tallest until the opening of the World Trade Center in 1972.

Over the decades, the iconic building fell on hard times. In 1995, after years of neglect and a string of owners, Donald Trump bought 40 Wall Street. He said he paid a mere million dollars, but that's probably not true. With Donald Trump, anything he says needs to be rigorously fact checked. He originally planned to convert the upper half to residential space, leaving the bottom half as commercial space. However, the cost of converting the top half to residential space proved to be too high, and so it remained an office building.

It was easy to see why Donald Trump bought the building and used it for his corporate headquarters. It was the address: 40 Wall Street. Doesn't it *sound* important? Doesn't it sound like it's part of the bedrock foundation of the American financial system? You can practically see the ghosts of J.P. Morgan and Cornelius Vanderbilt nodding in approval. What better address could be embossed on the gilt-edged letterhead of Trump University, or any other Trump business?

In fact, many New York insiders claim that 40 Wall Street is packed with characters who have found three irresistible enticements to locating a business there: a bona fide Wall Street address, low rent, and a landlord who has other preoccupations. The building's average annual rent per square foot is thirty-six dollars, about twenty dollars cheaper than the area's average asking price and less than half of Midtown's rates. As *Bloomberg* reported, since Trump took it over in 1995, the seventy-two-story building has housed "frauds, thieves, boiler rooms, and penny-stock schemers." According to the Securities and Exchange Commission's public alert list, no U.S. address has been home to more of the unregistered brokerages that investors complain about.

The elevator whisked me to the Trump offices on the thirty-second floor, where they had me wait in the conference room that looked like a set from *The Apprentice*. The room accommodated over twenty people around a huge mahogany conference table. Lining the walls were expansive bookshelves filled with all of Donald Trump's books and other books about real estate.

Then people began coming in. The supervisor came in first, then a CPA, then a marketing guy, then Michael Sexton, the CEO of Trump University, and then David Highbloom, the COO. More Trump advisors came into the room. They all looked prosperous, well-fed, and tough.

I anticipated a thrilling experience. Here I was, a scrappy guy from Pittston, Pennsylvania, surrounded by the opulent splendor of one of the most iconic buildings in New York, interviewing with some of the highest associates of the legendary king of real estate, the Midas of Manhattan, Donald J. Trump.

On that first day, I was interviewed by two or three people. After six hours of grilling, they asked me to come back the next day. I thought, *okay, we're making progress.* On the second day they sent in two or three more people. We talked and talked. So far, no actual *job title* or *position* had been specified. The only topic we discussed was real estate and what could be done legally in various states. They would pose real estate scenarios and I would have to resolve the issue or solve the puzzle, coming up with options and solutions. They would say, "What do you have, what's the escape clause for purchase and sales contracts?"

I came back for a third day, for another six hours of interrogation. The only things missing were the spotlight in my eyes and the rubber hose. I soon realized that my interrogators didn't know the correct answers because they were dutifully taking notes. The scene quickly became ridiculous. These people had no idea about real estate transactions. I felt like I had been brought there to train them!

As the week went on, I became disillusioned. The whole thing seemed like a pointless charade. Weren't these people supposed to be the best and the brightest? How on earth could any of them not know the basics of real estate law and procedures?

Despite my bewilderment, I stuck with the interviews. I suppose that after a while I was curious to see what the hell was going on. How would they end this thing? Would they offer me a job, or would they say, "Thanks, Steve, for spending a week of your valuable time with us.

We'll call you if we need you. Sandra will show you out." Could they really be that callous?

On Friday afternoon I was in the conference room with **five** other people. They included Michael Sexton, David Highbloom, and a man named Brad Schneider, whom I was to learn more about very soon. I was at the end of my rope. I wasn't taking care of my own business and I felt like I was being strung along.

I said, "What's it going to be? Should we call it a day?"

Sexton picked up a pad of Post-It notes and wrote something on it. He then slid it across the table to me. I thought it was a cheesy, B-movie gesture. *Seriously,* I thought, *you have to play these stupid games?* Being a good sport, I picked up the pad and looked at it. Written on the pad was a dollar amount: $72,500. I felt like I had been slapped across the face with a dead fish. Trying very hard not to lunge across the table to wring the punk's neck, I thought, what a ridiculous offer.

Then I realized that this was the opening gambit in a "negotiation." Donald Trump is all about "negotiating." For Trump, this means you make an opening offer so low it's insulting. While this may make you think you're being clever and tough, deeply offending the other guy has an unintended side effect: you forever poison the relationship.

You really think I'm worth only seventy-two thousand five hundred dollars a year? Yeah? Well, fuck you forever.

Even if you reach a deal—which we did—from that moment my opinion of the Trump people was that they were snakes. Looking him in the eye, I said, "Double it and we'll start talking."

Remember, there had not yet been one word about what my job would be. All I knew was that I would be working for Trump. In their world, what more did I need to know? Eventually, we made a deal. I'd get seventy-two thousand five hundred for the first three months as a trial period, at which point my salary would double to $143,000 a year.

They told me what the job was. They explained how Trump University worked: it was a school for students who wanted to learn real estate the Donald Trump way. To teach and sell the courses, they would be hiring a team of outside consultants as "mentors." I would be the primary in-house real estate expert, a representative on call to resolve coaching, mentoring, and student issues. Any student working on a real estate transaction could call the Trump University hotline, and I would answer the phone.

I had something Trump University needed. My expertise in real estate could not be denied.

But I needed them even more. And they knew that the housing crash was coming. They knew that there was only going to be a short period of time that Trump University could be successful. They knew they needed to strike quickly.

Despite the creepy vibe, I was seduced. I ignored the fact that although these people knew nothing about real estate, despite being the top brass of Trump University, an institute of "higher learning" that supposedly conveyed to its eager students the secrets of the real estate business as revealed by the master himself, Donald J. Trump. I was still an impressionable person at this stage in my life. I was eager to find someone to revere, and at Trump University I found the acceptance that I had craved since childhood. Somebody *believed* in me. The gates were opening and I was going to enter the exalted hallways of money and power. I was *in*.

4.

I had decided to hitch my future to a company that was not even three years old. The founding of Trump University can be traced to August 4, 2004, when Trump's attorney Jenifer deWolf Paine filed papers with the U.S. Patent and Trademark Office seeking to have the phrase TRUMP UNIVERSITY protected by law. The filing said that the company would provide "educational services in the nature of conducting on-line courses in the fields of business and real estate."

The online news service *The Smoking Gun* quickly sensed the potential for mockery. On August 26, they published a snarky article under the headline "The Donald As the Dean?":

Proving again that his megalomania knows no bounds, Donald Trump is plotting the establishment of, we kid you not, Trump University . . . . It is unclear what position Trump, a graduate of the Wharton School of Finance, will hold at Trump U. Perhaps he can lecture on the importance of having a rich father. Or maybe he could offer a somber Founder's Day reflection on how he actually managed to lose money operating a casino. Either way, TSG is looking forward to TU's first graduation ceremony, when Trump desperately tries to corral his squirrely 'do under a golden mortarboard.

The idea for Trump University had not come from Trump but from Michael Sexton, who eventually became the CEO. Sexton was a management consultant with a master's degree from Tuck School of Business at Dartmouth. In 2004, he approached Trump with the concept of licensing Trump's name for online education courses. As he said in a 2013 deposition, "In 2004, as a result of my prior experience studying and analyzing instructional training products for professionals, my then business partner and I began to explore the idea of developing instructional products for small business owners and individual entrepreneurs under the 'Donald Trump' brand. At the time, in addition to being renowned as a savvy and successful business owner and entrepreneur, Donald Trump also was featured in a very popular television program—*The Apprentice*—that not only was entertaining, but also provided instruction on Mr. Trump's business ideas and philosophy.

"Our concept was to build a world-class business under the Trump brand, focused on servicing the needs of small and midsized business owners through technology-based, practical instructional products. We focused on small and midsized business owners because we believed that entrepreneurs historically had been underserved by training and education companies up to that point in time in delivering practical, real-world instruction."

As for real estate, years later he claimed in a deposition that his only experience with real estate transactions had been buying his own home. This was interesting, because in 2010 he and I partnered up to purchase a house together at 66 Gerardi Avenue in Newport Beach, Rhode Island. It had three bedrooms and three baths, and we paid eighteen thousand dollars for it. And the check that Sexton wrote for the purchase was drawn on an LLC within another LLC. At the time, the arrangement struck me as being a pretty good way to obscure a paper trail.

Trump liked Sexton's idea of Trump University, and despite his oft-repeated belief that you should always use other people's money—OPM, as it's called—he offered to drop his own cash into the business. He agreed to fund Trump University, giving Sexton a stake in the company.

The project's timing was perfect, coinciding with two auspicious developments for the real estate tycoon: the nation's booming real estate market was giving hope to many who dreamed of striking it rich, and through his hit TV show *The Apprentice*, the billionaire was developing an image as America's greatest business expert.

By the end of 2004, Trump, Sexton, and Jonathan Spitalny, a Bear Stearns senior managing director who had helped connect the two, had hammered out an agreement in which Trump would own more than ninety percent of the business. Trump initially invested about $2 million, and he later invested more money. As the CEO of Trump University, Sexton was paid $250,000 per year and had a 4.5 percent ownership stake.

The grand opening announcement came on May 23, 2005 at a glitzy press conference in the grand lobby of Trump Tower. With Michael Sexton and other top executives by his side, Donald Trump outlined how Trump University would consist of online courses, CD-ROMs, and other learning programs for business professionals.

Bloomberg.com reported on the splashy unveiling. "The Donald launches his own online self-directed learning courses—and they differ mightily from the usual fare," wrote Brian Hindo.

"With business schools around the country using Donald Trump's reality TV vehicle *The Apprentice* as a teaching tool, perhaps it was just a matter of time before The Donald cut out the middleman. On May 23, the real estate mogul formally launched Trump University—a foray into the fast-growing field of online education. Courses are expected to begin as early as Thursday, May 25."

As Trump wrote (or, more precisely, as his ghostwriter Meredith McIver wrote) in his book *Trump 101: The Way to Success*:

Another purpose of this book is to introduce you to Trump University, which grew out of my desire to impart the business knowledge I accumulated over the years and to find a practical, convenient way to teach success. Trump University doesn't just bear my name; I'm actively involved in it. I participated in creating the curricula, and my words, ideas, and image have been woven into the courses we provide. I'm deeply and actively involved in Trump University because I firmly believe in the power of education and its function as an engine of success. I want to help people, and, simply put, the Trump University students want to be successful. I'm on their side.

Donald Trump appeared in a short video promoting his new venture. You can still see the video on YouTube—it's called "Trump University Intro." Donald Trump, standing before a wall of impressive-looking leather-bound books, looks straight into the camera and says, "At Trump University, we teach success. That's what it's all about: success. It's going to happen to you."

The scene then cuts to photos of skyscrapers. Over a soundtrack of big triumphant chords, the narrator, a guy who sounds like God, intones, "Donald Trump is without question the world's most famous businessman. As a real estate developer, he has reshaped the New York skyline with some of that city's most prestigious and elegant buildings. Donald Trump brings his years of experience to the world of business education with the launch of Trump University."

Then back to Trump: "If you're going to achieve anything, you have to take *action*," he says. "And action is what Trump University is all about. But action is just a small part of Trump University. Trump University is about knowledge, about a lot of different things. Above all, it's about how to become successful."

Then we see Trump seated, with an old-fashioned globe at his elbow, facing a man who is "interviewing" him. The smiling guy looks like a friendly Cocker Spaniel eager to be patted on the head by his master. This is Jon Ward, about whom his website says, "As a business educator Jon masterminded all the initial education programs for Trump University, and conducted a full-length video interview with Donald Trump."

In the video, Trump tells Ward:

We're going to have professors, and adjunct professors that are absolutely terrific, terrific people, terrific brains. Successful. We are going to have the best of the best. And honestly, if you don't learn from them, if you don't learn from me, if you don't learn from the people that we're going to be putting forward—*and these are all people that are hand-picked by me*—then you're just not going to make it in terms of the world of success.

I think the biggest step towards success is going to be: Sign up at Trump University.

We're going to teach you about business, we're going to teach you better than the business schools are going to teach you—and I went to the best business school—we're going to teach you better, it's going to be a shorter process, it's not going to involve years and years of your life, it's going to be less expensive, and I think it's going to be a better education.

We're also going to make sure that no matter what you do, as I said before, you're going to love it. Because if you don't love it, it's never ever going to work.

The claim Trump made was crystal clear: the instructors would be *hand-picked* by Trump himself. It was an assertion that he would later come to regret.

The promotional materials for Trump University revealed that the company wouldn't be offering degrees or traditional classroom instruction. The school would have no textbooks, no lectures, and no grades. And despite the explicit promise of hand-picked instructors, there would not even be teachers in the ordinary sense.

Instead, the education plan was to provide short, focused lessons in specific subjects that emphasized practice over theory. The first three courses would be available to students at $300 per course. These would be introductions to real estate, to marketing, and to entrepreneurship. Students would be divided into groups of six to twelve and could choose to complete the courses in either one or two weeks.

Students would log on to trumpuniversity.com to get their "Empire City" assignments. For example, entrepreneurship students would be asked to assume the role of a venture capitalist and analyze a business plan. They would then submit their work to classmates for a peer review. A course would consist of three such assignments.

"People have learned the hard way that . . . trying to replicate the classroom experience isn't particularly effective," said Michael Sexton, a man lacking substantive educational credentials, about the online learning concept.

"Education is worthless without feedback. This system enables however many students we have to get live feedback about their work. . . . This is not for somebody who wants to put a sheepskin on the wall and thinks that is going to meaningfully help their career."

What a breathtakingly brazen scheme! Why have teachers, whom you have to pay, when you could instead have the students critique each other's work? With this low-cost system, the students would receive "live feedback," as Sexton called it, from other students who knew no more about the subject than their peers did. Trump University's brand of "self-directed learning" was a departure from most accredited online education programs that offered self-direction bolstered by regular, personal feedback from a qualified instructor.

Trump assured the assembled members of the press that students wouldn't be left to wander unguided in the academic forest. The Trump University website would have some background material for students to peruse, an "Expert Center," which featured clickable videos of the professors, and even video appearances by Donald Trump himself, offering occasional nuggets of wisdom.

Within a month, Sexton said, business school professors would be available to students via an online bulletin board, and eventually the professors would write feedback on the final assignment of each course. Trump wouldn't be reading any term papers, but Sexton said the tycoon would hold periodic live online Q&A sessions with students and would also address questions through an "Ask Mr. Trump" feature.

To bolster its claims to legitimacy, Trump University hired an educator with significant academic credentials as its Chief Learning Officer, Roger Schank, Ph.D. Schank was a renowned artificial intelligence theorist, cognitive psychologist, learning scientist, educational reformer, and entrepreneur who had founded the Institute for the Learning Sciences at Northwestern University and was chief executive of Socratic Arts, which specialized in curriculum design. Beginning in the late 1960s, he had pioneered conceptual dependency theory (within the context of natural language understanding) and case-based reasoning, both of which challenged cognitivist views of memory and reasoning. In short, he was a real intellectual. He was pretty much the exact opposite of Sexton and Trump.

"The problem with school is that school is a little academic, a little theoretical, not really practical," said Schank at the press event. "We want to give people experience."

With its extremely do-it-yourself structure, what Trump University proposed to deliver was almost like a living version of a best-selling business book such as *Rich Dad, Poor Dad*. John Vogel, an adjunct professor at Dartmouth College's Tuck School of Business, stood by Trump's side at the news conference. He had recorded video lectures on topics such as variable versus fixed-rate mortgages and how to weigh the pros and cons of different properties for an online Trump University course directed at would-be real-estate investors. He reportedly earned $1,800 for a day's work while recording the sessions. He later said he spent his paycheck on a wide-screen television.

On June 1, 2005, *The Dartmouth*, which is the Dartmouth College student newspaper ("America's oldest college newspaper—founded 1799") ran a congratulatory article featuring Professor Vogel. Under the headline "Tuck professor aids Trump University," reporter Kevin Garland wrote, "Tuck Business School professor John Vogel recently teamed up with Donald Trump and Tuck graduate Michael Sexton TU '04 to create an online course for the new Trump University. '*The Apprentice* is an education show,' Vogel said in reference to the viciously competitive NBC reality program. 'There was an opportunity to expand that educational mission by creating online courses. Donald liked the idea and hired Michael Sexton to do it.'"

It was Sexton who recruited Vogel to create this real estate course. He chose Vogel because of his reputation in the business real estate academic sector, his peer recommendations, and Sexton's "great memories of professor Vogel as a teacher." For his part, Vogel emphasized the need for sound academics to help jump-start Trump University. "Sexton's thought was that Donald Trump has many brilliant ideas," Vogel told *The Dartmouth*, "but is not the type of person who is going to sit down and design a course. He doesn't have time or a lot of experience in developing courses, so he was looking for someone who does have experience."

Jack Kaplan, a Columbia Business School adjunct professor, helped develop the original entrepreneurship course. "It's exciting to work for this guy," Kaplan told a *New York Daily News* reporter at the event, referring to Trump. "I hope I don't get fired."

Another recruit was Karen Slavick-Lennard, who had managed a robotics lab before becoming a project manager and content developer at Trump University in April 2005. "I was never comfortable with the fact that it was called Trump University," she later told the *Wall Street Journal*. "But we were making really good quality, useful stuff for people trying to take control over their own lives and have their own businesses." As an example of the quality of the Trump University product, she cited a simulation of a city that immersed students in realistic real-estate transactions. Trump knew that he had hired real talent. "These guys are getting paid too much," he joked at the press event.

A six-part audio and DVD course called *The Wealth Builder's Blueprint* was for sale on the website, and Sexton said orders had been rolling in even before the official launch. No students had been enrolled yet, but Sexton expected the publicity from the gala announcement to draw enough students in time for the start of classes later that week. At the outset, Trump University was going after a niche that fell somewhere between pragmatic adult education and aspirational learning for white-collar workers. The course content differed from accredited degree programs and vocational training provided by other major online players. The pricing was significantly lower, and the coursework and experience was quite different than the typical business school executive education offerings.

Much was at stake for Trump: unlike many of his past ventures, he had funded Trump University all by himself. Sexton said the expectation was that the unit would turn a profit by the end of the year.

Looking ahead, Trump and Sexton had big plans. Three more course offerings were on their way within the next few months: Negotiations, Leadership, and Business Communication. More advanced versions of the existing subjects were also on tap. "On top of that," said Sexton, "we'll start building not accredited curriculum but services, whether it's coaching services, or mentoring, or consulting." Many of the inquiries had been coming from outside the United States, which made him enthusiastic about overseas expansion.

While hardly a university, the company's business model was not without merit. If in fact students had access to Donald Trump—even via web conference—and the curriculum conveyed real information, three hundred bucks a course was not a bad deal. And Trump's motives seemed sincere—or at least as sincere as a shark's motivations could be. Trump University would be a noble endeavor, he said, with an emphasis on education over profits. It was a way for him to give back, to share his expertise with the masses, to build a "legacy as an educator."

He claimed that he wouldn't even keep all the money. If he happened to make a profit, he would turn the funds over to charity. "If I had a choice of making lots of money or imparting lots of knowledge, I think I'd be as happy to impart knowledge as to make money," Trump announced at the press event.

Ads touted Trump University as "the next best thing to being Trump's apprentice." "Priceless information" would help attendees build wealth in the same real estate game that made Trump rich. If only it were true.

The New York State Department of Education was not impressed by the glitz and glamour. A few days after Trump and Sexton announced the grand opening, the agency sent a letter to Trump, Sexton, and Trump University saying that they were violating state law by using the word "university" when in fact Trump University was not actually chartered as a university and did not have the required license to offer live instruction or training. Although Sexton promised that the organization would stop instructing students in New York, the substance of the letter was ignored. The name Trump University remained, and the address of 40 Wall Street, New York, stayed on the gilded letterhead.

5.

For the next two years, Trump University made an effort to maintain standards of quality in its online offerings. There were attempts to provide legitimate information to consumers, and, since Donald Trump was a master of marketing, the university's online presence was bolstered by traditional books, which Trump was an expert at selling.

On April 1, 2006, John Wiley & Sons published *Trump University Real Estate 101: Building Wealth with Real Estate Investments* by Gary W. Eldred, Ph.D., with a foreword by Donald J. Trump. This was a real book written by a real expert. Eldred had written or co-written several college textbooks and many academic articles and research papers, and had held faculty positions in the graduate business programs of Stanford, the University of Illinois, and the University of Virginia. The advertising copy for *Real Estate 101* said:

> Trump University books are practical, straightforward primers on the basics of doing business the Trump way—successfully. Each book is written by a leading expert in the field and includes an inspiring foreword by Trump himself.

Key ideas throughout are illustrated by real-life examples from Trump and other senior executives in the Trump organization. Perfect for anyone who wants to get ahead in business without the MBA, these streetwise books provide real-world business advice based on the one thing readers can't get in any business school—experience.

Eldred's book *Investing in Real Estate* was blurbed by Michael Sexton himself: "Donald Trump and I have created Trump University to offer the highest quality, success-driven education available. Our one goal is to help professionals build their careers, businesses, and wealth. That's why we selected Gary Eldred to help us develop our first courses in real estate investing. His books stand out for their knowledge-packed content and success-driven advice."

Trump University "101" print books and audio books included *Trump University Commercial Real Estate 101: How Small Investors Can Get Started and Make It Big*, by David Lindahl (also with a foreword by Donald J. Trump), and *Trump University Entrepreneurship 101: How to Turn Your Idea into a Money Machine*, by Michael E. Gordon (Donald J. Trump apparently contributed nothing to this one). Other "101" titles covered marketing, branding, and asset protection.

Trump University also produced a flood of CD audiobooks. One was *Branding for Profit* by Donald Trump, Jon Ward, and James Burgin. It's still available on Amazon.com. You can buy a new copy for forty bucks. Released on October 5, 2006, the breathless—and strangely garbled—promotional text reads:

Do you know how to market and brand for maximum profit? Donald Trump sure does. And now, Donald

Trump—and his hand-picked experts, James Burgin and Jon Ward—are teaming up to share their branding expertise with you. Now, you can. Introducing 'Branding for Profit: Build Your Brand to Increase Sales and Customer Loyalty.' Donald Trump, James Burgin and Jon Ward know how to do it. They'll show you how in a blockbuster home study series (CD/workbook). Order today—and succeed the Trump Way!

Another 2006 CD audiobook was *Real Estate Goldmine: How to Get Rich Investing in Pre-Foreclosures*, by Donald Trump and Gary Eldred. It begins with a monologue by Trump, who says, "We're not peddling get-rich-quick schemes, no blue-sky promises or an easy road to riches." But he pledges that his course will offer a "real estate gold mine." Then Jon Ward interviews real estate investment adviser Gary Eldred about the best strategies for taking advantage of homeowners facing foreclosures. Throughout the course, Eldred provides a variety of techniques for spotting homes that are in pre-foreclosure—for instance, by looking for an owner who is delinquent on payments—and he offers strategies for persuading owners to sell their homes at a discount when they're facing foreclosure.

In a voice tinged with sadness, Eldred notes several times that foreclosures are a painful but inevitable part of the economy. Trump makes a similar point in his introduction. "The sad fact is, more and more property owners are getting themselves in trouble," Trump says. "Defaulting on mortgages and losing their homes or commercial properties. I'm sorry for them, but life goes on, and the fact is, one person's misfortune is someone else's opportunity. That's just the way the world works. This program shows you how to make a lot of money from investing in pre-foreclosures."

Eldred covers how to take advantage of short sales—a deal in which the net proceeds from selling the property will fall short of the debts secured by liens against the property. In common terms, it's when you buy a property that's "underwater," which means the owner owes more than the property is worth. In this case, if all lien holders agree to accept less than the amount owed on the debt, the sale of the property can be accomplished. Eldred points out that a key aspect of such a transaction is convincing a lender that the owner won't be able to pay back the loan as it stands. The goal, Eldred says, is to find homeowners who are in a truly desperate financial position.

"Under no circumstance will a lender accept a short sale if they think they can squeeze that borrower for an extra nickel, so certified destitution evidence needs to be included," he explains. He lists the conditions that are ideal for a short sale: "The borrower is out of work, the borrower has fifty thousand dollars in unpaid medical claims, the borrower is completely disabled, the borrower has an extraordinarily messy divorce where everything has been squandered." This was tough, bare-knuckled stuff. Illegal? No. Nice? Not at all.

While it was not an actual university, and while its promotional material sounded like it had been written by a fifth grader, Trump University appeared to be striving for respectability, with the ambition to deliver actual usable information to students. Not for long.

With sudden swiftness, in late 2006 and early 2007, Trump U. changed course. The online courses and Ivy League instructors were tossed aside in favor of a new business model of presenting live workshops that taught attendees how to strike it rich in the real estate business.

The new business model was designed to operate in two stages: first, offering aspiring real-estate magnates a free ninety-minute "Profit from Real Estate Orientation" (also known as the "Preview") where they'd be pressured to pay for the second stage: a three-day "Profit from Real Estate Workshop." During the workshop, they'd be enticed and cajoled into buying one of the "Trump Elite Packages," which were offered at three price points: $9,995 (Bronze), $19,495 (Silver), and then, the whopper, at $34,995 (Trump Gold Elite).

It didn't stop there. During the Gold Elite program, there was constant pressure to purchase other Trump University affiliate programs and products, varying in price from $495 to $9,995. As a result, students could ultimately spend upwards of seventy thousand dollars—all as the result of being lured in by the free "Profit from Real Estate Orientation."

The professional educators, who had been hired with such great fanfare in May 2005, were dismissed. Chief Learning Officer Roger Schank was told the school had used up the three million dollars that Trump had invested in the project, and that his services were no longer needed.

"They put a certain amount of money into it and then the money stopped, suddenly," he told *The Daily Beast*. "I said, 'What happened?' And they said, 'Well, we just don't have any more money, and we need to make money quickly in some other way.' And that was kind of the end. In its initial stages, its initial setup, the school was genuine, it was good. When they started doing real estate workshops, I just wondered about it... Maybe he didn't have that much money. That was my thought at the time. There was a lot of pressure about money and discussion, 'Well, we only have three million dollars to start.'"

Dartmouth professor John Vogel also left the company. "Had I realized they were going to change course from providing high-quality online education to something that was closer to a boiler room operation and these 'how to get rich' seminars, I never would have gotten involved," he later told *The Wall Street Journal.*

Karen Slavick-Lennard said that in early 2007, as the company moved to presenting live workshops, her role changed from creating course content to serving as an event planner. She organized two early sessions, in Miami and in Los Angeles, but she left a few months later, saying that the work was "not fulfilling." She saw Trump and his daughter Ivanka visit the office only once. "The man is a walking billboard for himself," she said. "It's like he walks around selling himself. That's how he talks. I found it really bizarre."

Ronald Schackenberg served as a sales manager at Trump University from October 2006 through May 2007. He worked out of 40 Wall Street, selling Trump University programs to consumers who called to inquire and at live events. He stated in a 2012 deposition, "Around February 2007, the direction of Trump University's business drastically changed to 'live events' and seminars driven by high-pressure front-end salesmen, inexperienced in real estate, making high-pressure sales. If consumers attended the event and did not purchase a seminar, the Trump University sales team followed up with them. Trump University's live seminars and events were not based on Gary Eldred's Real Estate Investor Training

Program. Instead, Mark Dove, who essentially owns that 'front-end high-pressure speaker scam' world, provided speakers, instructors, mentors, and salespeople to Trump University, and these people brought with them their own programs, which turned into Trump University programs. I was very uncomfortable with this new direction of business, as I believed it to be very unethical."

Within a year after his departure, Adam Eisenstat, who worked in marketing for Trump University between spring 2005 and spring 2006, said he didn't recognize the company. "It didn't resemble anything that I was familiar with," he told the *Wall Street Journal.* "It seemed like a separate company."

Another salesperson, Jason Nicholas, who worked for Trump University from May through October 2007 at 40 Wall Street, stated in his 2012 deposition, "Trump University salespeople, including me, uniformly told consumers, from the script, that they would 'work with Donald Trump's real estate experts' and that these instructors were 'experts in today's real estate world and will teach all of the non-traditional or unconventional ways of buying and selling real estate.'" This was not true. Most of the Trump University instructors and mentors were not experts in real estate and did not have experience in the real estate techniques they were teaching. They were unqualified people posing as Donald Trump's "right-hand men." They were teaching methods that were unethical, and they had had little to no experience flipping properties or doing real estate deals.

Some of the managers misrepresented their qualifications. For example, Manager Paul Quintal, who was in charge of the entire Trump University sales team and live events, said he had an MBA, when actually he did not have an MBA.

Trump University told consumers that Donald Trump would be actively involved in Trump University. But as far as I could tell, Donald Trump was not actively involved in Trump University. In the time that I worked at Trump University, I only saw Donald Trump come in one time, for five to ten minutes, to see Michael Sexton; he didn't talk with or interact with anyone else, as far as I could see, and his bodyguard wouldn't even permit Trump University employees to shake his hand.

Tad Lignell was one of the new mentors who came to Trump University through an association with Mark Dove. Lignell lives in Utah and has a personal interest in real estate—he told *Rolling Stone* he owns several rental properties and regularly "flips" houses for a profit—but he has no formal education or any kind of license. His background, like most of the other mentors and speakers, was in motivational speaking.

Lignell told *Rolling Stone* that he knew Mark Dove prior to joining Trump University, but he couldn't say for sure if it was Dove who brought him on board. "The seminar business is kind of a small world. People know each other, so when Trump was building his business or starting his business, they were looking for a team," he said.

As for learning the supposedly exclusive Trump system, Lignell said, "We had some training and we had their manuals and stuff, but, you know, there wasn't a strict guideline that told us how to operate. We had basically PowerPoints of the things we were to cover."

He had little contact with 40 Wall Street. "I wasn't really connected with the office," he said, "with the exception of them sending me a list of new students."

Despite the courses being eliminated from Trump University, the audiobooks were not taken down from Amazon.com. Here's an interesting comment from a customer who gave *Real Estate Goldmine: How to Get Rich Investing in Pre-Foreclosures* a rating of one star out of five. The review is dated October 20, 2008 (as of this writing, you can still see it on the Amazon page): "There is a fairly good audio presentation by Gary Eldred, Ph.D. There is no twelve-month study course. The web site has not been updated since March 2007, and the course essentially does not exist."

Initially, the live programming was farmed out to a company called Business Strategies Group LLC, which licensed the Trump name. The owners of that outside firm, Irene and Michael Milin, have been investigated by attorneys general of multiple states for their programs promising ways to make money through real estate and by getting government grants. According to court documents, they continued operating Trump courses until about 2008, although beginning in 2007, Trump University had launched its own workshops in-house.

As Michael Sexton stated in his August 2013 deposition to the New York attorney general, "Our plan was to contract with one of these companies to launch a live event business to meet what we understood to be a demand in the marketplace for that. As part of that process we would try to learn everything we could about what it took to run this kind of business successfully. You know, kind of a good—what we felt they were doing good and what we felt we could improve upon, and at some point it was our idea to bring it back in-house once we felt confident that we understood the business and not just the economics of it but every component of it."

According to Corinne Sommer, Trump University's manager of the Events Department from May through October 2007, the first Trump University live event took place in Florida in May of 2007, and the second one took place in Los Angeles, California approximately one month later. Before these two live events, Trump University courses were only offered online. These two live events had approximately five hundred attendees each—a very auspicious beginning. The program was green-lighted, and after that, Trump University held live workshops nearly every week in different areas of the country.

From Trump's perspective—as a guy who cared only about maximizing revenues—it made sense to pour resources into the live workshop business model and away from the online model. When you think about it, an online business is not something that makes sense for Donald Trump. An online school depends on its customers taking action themselves. They need to find the store—or, rather, the "university"—and purchase its product. If the customers decide to cancel or do something else, there's not much the online storeowner can do about it.

Donald Trump didn't have any control over his online customers. They sat at their computers in their own homes, and while he could try to upsell them with persuasive sales pages, it was not a very efficient money machine. Trump was too impatient for that. He wanted something he could scale up and that would allow him and his people to have much more control. The live workshops allowed the sales team to herd actual human beings into a room and give them a scientifically prepared hard sell. In the room, the salespeople had much more psychological sway.

The online business model is like fishing with a rod and reel. You put your baited hook in the water and hope a fish will notice it and swim over. If the fish ignores the hook, there's nothing you can do about it. You can sit there for hours and never get a nibble. If there's one thing Donald Trump hates to do, it is waiting for a fish to swim over and nibble. He wants to *go out and get the fish*.

The workshop business is like taking a big eighty-foot trawler out in the ocean and casting a huge net. You scoop up everything that swims into the net. You haul the net on deck and dump the fish into a big pile. Then you sort through the fish. You throw back the worthless ones—in this case, the ones who have no money. You keep the valuable ones—the ones who might be able to pony up $35,000 for the Trump Gold Elite package. Casting a big net sure beats sitting on the dock with your hook in the water, waiting for a nibble.

6.

By the middle of 2007, Trump University was running three-day workshops in Phoenix, Orlando, Las Vegas, and other cities, with titles like "Fast Track to Foreclosure" and "Quick Turn Real Estate." The workshops often included advice on the different types of foreclosures, how to identify promising investments, and some hands-on practice on contacting property owners to discuss an investment.

In the early days of the live events, the format wasn't set in stone. As Sexton testified in 2013, "We had had other event formats. We could do a one-day event. We could do a three-day free event or a two-day free event. We experimented with different models."

In regard to the instructors and the curriculum, Michael Sexton testified in his deposition that Donald Trump was not involved. Sexton stated under oath that no one at the Trump Organization, including Donald Trump, reviewed the curriculum materials or was aware of who was being hired to lead the live events. He said, "None of our instructors at the live events were hand-picked by Donald Trump." When asked by attorney Melvin Goldberg if Donald Trump participated in the creation of the materials used in the three-day real estate workshops, Sexton replied, "No, he did not."

Of course this is absolutely contrary to every assertion that Trump University made in its advertising and marketing, including claims made by the instructors themselves in front of their impressionable and trusting students. The major selling point of Trump University was that Donald Trump himself was the guiding spirit.

Financially, he was *very* involved. From the start, the business was intertwined with the conglomerate Trump Organization, which controls other Trump companies. Donald Trump was one of the few signatories on Trump University checks, along with his children and Trump Organization chief financial officer Allen Weisselberg. At least one of them was required to sign each check written by Trump University. In a 2009 email exchange about paying $15,000 for a radio campaign in New York, for example, former Trump University controller Steven Matejek explained that after they were cut, "checks then always go to Trump Org for final review and signature."

How about the advertising copy that implied Donald Trump had personal oversight over the school and its programs? Michael Sexton testified, "He would always see the ad copy . . . . He personally approved all the ads that were in the newspaper."

Once the money from workshops started rolling in, Trump repaid himself the funds that he invested, plus several million more in capital distributions. Despite Trump's grandiose announcements at the grand opening event at Trump Tower, there was no record of a single penny going to charity.

According to *Politico*, expenses, including automobile insurance, were covered by the larger Trump Organization, as were IT services. The school rented its space from the Trump Building at 40 Wall Street in New York—and famously used the address on its letterhead—and the Trump Organization handled retirement plans for Trump University staff. From the point of view of finances, Trump was deeply connected to the business, even if he wasn't making most hiring decisions or speaking at events.

From 2007 until 2010, it seemed the focus for Trump University was purely on separating suckers from their money. Prospects called a phone number or signed up online, and a few days later they received "exclusive" free tickets in the mail. The tickets were impressively signed in gold by Donald J. Trump. At the free Preview, one of the first tasks of the Trump salesperson was to qualify each prospect. This was done by observing the prospect's behavior and by having the prospect fill out a financial disclosure form. The goal was to learn as much as possible about the financial condition of the prospect so they could be coached to produce the highest possible fee. At the same time, the event leader would guide the participants through a carefully orchestrated set of steps designed to elicit a purchase.

After the "free Preview," if you were willing to pay, you would be invited to attend the three-day workshop, usually held at a hotel ballroom, for which the price tag was $1,495. Each "Profit From Real Estate Workshop" had a designated speaker and a team of staffers, who led breakout sessions, facilitated the events, and pressured participants to buy the most expensive Trump Elite packages they could afford. Participants who purchased the three-day workshop did so with the understanding that they would be exposed to Trump's personal secrets of real estate trading. But in reality, they got very little, and were promised that the real secrets would be revealed to those who forked over more money for the Trump Elite mentorship programs.

As I said before, the Trump Elite programs came in three levels: Bronze, Silver, and Trump Gold Elite, with prices ranging from $9,995 to $34,995. The Trump Gold Elite package, which was the very best you could get, included some impressive benefits:

IN-FIELD MENTORSHIP

Nothing can accelerate a real estate investment more than having a Trump Mentor. Our Mentors fly into your market and in three action-packed days walk you through every step of a real estate transaction, from finding great properties to running the numbers to making the offers. You work hand in hand with the Mentor to learn how to invest the Trump way so that even when the Mentor is gone, you can continue to build your financial future.

ADVANCED TRAINING RETREATS

Wealth Preservation Retreat

Learn how to choose the proper entity for your real estate or other business, structure yourself for lower taxes, protect yourself from frivolous lawsuits, and pass your wealth on to your heirs while protecting them from financial threats. You will learn directly from an experienced team including an attorney, accountant and investor.

Quick Start Real Estate Profits Retreat

Create immediate and monthly cash flow without using any of your own money or credit. You will learn how to wholesale, lease option, and owner-finance properties for quick profits.

Commercial & Multi-Family Retreat
Learn how to locate and analyze multi-unit properties by completing due diligence and learning market trends. You will learn: tax strategies, condo conversions, preconstruction, property management and more.

Creative Financing Retreat
Learn that creative financing can be more important than the money and credit you may or may not have. This retreat will teach you about financial statements, loan request packages, financing techniques, hard money connections, 1031 real estate exchanges, note techniques and much more . . . everything you will need to put deals together and get them closed.

TOOLS AND RESOURCES
Incorporate Your Business
If you are serious about investing in real estate or starting a new venture, you need to know about the many advantages of incorporating your business. The security that comes from forming an LLC cannot be underestimated, but the process can be confusing and time consuming. Trump University's LLC formation service handles your incorporation so that you can focus on building your business.

One-Year Membership: Foreclosure DealSource
This powerful foreclosure-finding tool gives you complete access to two million-plus constantly updated and refreshed distressed property listings throughout the United States. You'll get listings before they hit the open market–and

before the competition can get a jump on your profit-making plans. You will find and buy foreclosed properties at incredibly low prices—often for pennies on the dollar!

Wealth Builder's Network (WBN)
Premium Membership in the WBN is an exceptional learning resource that will educate and advise you on what it takes to be successful—Trump style! Premium members have access to weekly online classes and webinars; a 24/7 Q&A answers resource; an interactive investing program; a comprehensive resource library; and much more.

Real Estate Investor's Training Online Program (REIT)
This course provides focused training covering all aspects of the business. Comprised of four interactive courses, real-world simulation, and learning materials, this program is a powerful way for you to start investing your way to monumental wealth in the shortest time possible

According to sales documents, the actual "retail value" of the Trump Gold Elite package was $48,574. The value of the 3-Day In-Field Mentorship alone was $25,995. Prospects were assured that by virtue of their association with the workshop, by paying $34,995 they'd get a very special discount of over thirty percent.

As a point of comparison, when discussing the value of his school, Donald Trump often implied that Trump University somehow inhabited the same educational universe as Harvard University. In terms of *cost*, he was not far off. According to the Harvard website, the total 2015-2016 cost of tuition at Harvard College, without financial aid, was $45,278—actually *less* than the so-called retail value of the Trump Gold Elite package. And unlike Trump University, which was strictly a cash-in-advance business, Harvard offered generous scholarships to families who couldn't afford to pay full freight. At Harvard, families with students on scholarship paid an average of $11,500 annually toward the cost of a Harvard education. That's for a *full year* of Harvard instruction, not just a bunch of seminars and a three-day mentorship.

In a 2012 deposition, when asked about advertising claims that "there's money to be made" for students who attend Trump University, Donald Trump showed scant regard for the venerable institution on the banks of the Charles River: "They say go to Harvard, great school, blah, blah, blah, and I think it is—except I think we have a higher approval rating than Harvard, if you want to know the truth."

Interestingly, the speakers were eager to unload Gold Elite packages at huge discounts. A student named Kathleen Meese swore in her 2012 affidavit that three years earlier she had attended a three-day workshop at the Hyatt Place Saratoga in Malta, New York. Steve Goff was one of the speakers; the other two were Tiffany Brinkman and Scott Leitzell. According to Meese, "While the other Trump instructors spoke to the class, Mr. Goff pulled people aside one by one and told us that we would make money faster if we enrolled in Trump Elite programs and worked with a personal mentor. Mr. Goff asked if I could come up with twenty-five thousand dollars to sign up for the Gold Elite program. I told him I had a credit card with a thirty- thousand-dollar limit, but I did not want to pay that much for the Trump Gold Elite program. I told Mr. Goff that I could not fly to the Trump Elite seminars because I have a son with Down's syndrome who needs to be close to the hospital in case he needs to receive his medical treatments."

Steve Goff guaranteed Kathleen Meese that she would make back her $25,000 within sixty days, and that he would work with her personally. With great misgivings, Meese signed the credit card receipt and was charged twenty-five thousand dollars.

Three days later—after the cash was securely stashed in Trump's vaults—Steve Goff called Meese and told her that unfortunately he was not going to be her personal mentor. A man named Medith Webb, a realtor from Oklahoma City, would be providing her mentorship. Meese demanded an immediate refund. She received a call from Trump University program director Jason Schauer, but she did not get her money back.

In my opinion, the key question is: how could Steve Goff sell a product valued at nearly $35,000 at such a deep discount? He could do so because Trump University had no intention of delivering what it promised. In the world of Donald Trump, if you can get $25,000 out of a sucker and give them pennies in return, you're a fool if you don't do it.

The focus of all of the live workshops was not education. It seemed it was upselling—always pressuring the prospect to spend more and more. In the "profile" surveys that Trump University Team Members (as they were called) completed on their first day, participants would outline their financial goals, as well as their current assets and liabilities. Students were told that the information would help them determine how much they had on hand to invest in real estate.

But on that first day, after the workshop concluded, team members were instructed to use the information to rank each participant according to assets they had available to spend on more Trump University programs. Students were steered toward the most expensive Elite program that they could possibly afford, including by using such strategies as calling their bank, getting a credit card limit increase, and then maxing out the card. The sales procedures used by team members were dictated by the *Trump University Sales Play Book*.

This 172-page document spelled out in precise detail the setup and execution of events. In all fairness, anyone who has been involved in a franchise or sales program knows that playbooks are ubiquitous. They are how the head office instructs the company's representatives or franchisees how to sell the product, how to set up the storefront, or how to run an event. For example, the McDonald's playbook specifies everything that an individual McDonald's restaurant needs to do to conform to corporate standards. The playbook specifies everything from the exact color of the logo used in advertising to the greeting used by the server behind the counter.

What's interesting about the *Trump University Sales Play Book* is that its focus is purely on sales. The concept of Trump University as a source of education for the common good is nowhere to be found. Instead, what the playbook delineates is a good old-fashioned *hard sell*, worthy of the most slippery snake oil salesman of the Wild West.

The first ninety-seven pages of the playbook outline the usual administrative stuff: how to book the hotel for the workshop, how to set up the function room, what the team members must wear, and how a team member gets reimbursed for mileage on their car. This mind-numbing content would be familiar to anyone who has ever had the job of representing a big corporation in the field. There's instruction about how to qualify prospects, which should be done on the evening of the first day of the three-day workshop, on page 36:

> Once you have the completed profiles, the team should go through each profile and determine who has the most and least liquid assets and rank them using the following scale:
>
> E1 – Over $35,000 of liquid assets
> E2 – Between $20,000 and $30,000 of liquid assets
> E3 – Under $10,000 of liquid assets
> E4 – Less than $2,000 of liquid assets
> 401ks and IRAs should not be considered when using the ranking system since these are not liquid, available cash.

This ranking of incoming students by income is not something that most colleges and universities do. But then again, Trump University was nothing like a real college.

The chapters that begin on page ninety-eight show the team member how to *sell*. The instructions are precise and powerful. The chapters begin with a description of the psychology of the sales process:

> There are a variety of models used to develop a selling strategy. The common factor of all sales strategies is the most well-known model, the AIDA model:
> Attention/Interest/Desire/Action.
> Attention: Engage the potential customer so that they will want to talk. This can be done by identifying a

need the customer has or an opportunity in which they are interested.

Interest: Continue the discussion with the potential customer so that they will come to understand that you have a viable solution for their need.

Desire: Persuade the potential customer that your solution to their need is the best opportunity available.

Action: Ask for the enrollment–go for the "close."

With these instructions, team members were trained to lead the prospect step-by-step into the sales funnel and get them to fork over their credit card. Here's more:

Remember That They Are At The Preview Because They Want Something:

- Attendees want to be a part of Trump University and go to the three-Day Training [sic]. They only have fear or doubt they can do it stopping them from getting what they want. Money is never a reason for not enrolling in Trump University; if they really believe in you and your product, they will find the money. You are not doing any favor by letting someone use lack of money as an excuse.

Always Assume They Want To Go To The Workshop– Because Everyone Does:

- Understand that if someone says: "I don't want to go to the training," they are really saying: "I'm not used to dropping $995 on training and because it is new to me, I'm scared."

Experience Is On Our Side:

- Because we decide what happens in the training, an attendee must react to what we say. They don't have a choice. For example, we can spend hours and hours planning a question that they must deal with and give an answer to within seconds. We also have the advantage of testing the question out on hundreds of people and adjusting it to increase our chances for a desirable response. The attendee does not have the luxury of "practicing" his or her answer. However, we are losing this advantage if we don't take time to develop what we say and consciously practice what we say.

Master The Art Of Persuasion:

- The most persuasive words in the English language according to a study by the Psychology Department of Yale University are: You, New, Money, Easy, Discovery, Free, Results, Health, Save, Proven, Guarantee, and Love. They share three characteristics: they are simple, familiar and dramatic.

This was the company I had decided to join—but I wasn't shown any of this stuff. I never saw the *Trump University Sales Play Book*. I was asked to take over the online programs, which still had the lingering patina of respectability. Unfortunately, Gary Eldred, Roger Schank, John Vogel, Karen Slavick-Lennard, and the other professional educators were gone. I didn't know it at the time, but I was the only real estate expert at Trump University. And to think the bastards had originally offered me a measly $72,500 a year! I could have gotten that kind of money teaching real estate classes at a community college in the swamps of Florida.

Trump University hired me on a Friday and they wanted me to show up for work the following Monday. Due to Gary Eldred's impending departure, I became the adjunct professor with the title "in-house real estate expert coach and mentor." I was the only in-house real estate expert, and I held these licenses: correspondent lender, MBB, MB, and broker. Eldred stayed to train me for three months. He's brilliant in academia for real estate and a genuinely nice person. I was surprised at how much more I learned when he took me under his wing.

My supervisor was Brad Schneider, the director of service and sales. He was twenty-six and had been hired in October 2006. His previous job had been as national sales manager for graduate sales at Kaplan Test Prep and Admissions. His resume says that he "supervised and motivated a team of twelve sales advisors responsible for over $35 million of incoming revenue. . . Managed and maintained excellent customer service through direct communication with customers ensuring the highest level of customer satisfaction." Not much about either real estate or education in there. A lot about sales, though.

Nevertheless, I agreed to join Trump University because they were offering me the opportunity to provide accurate information to their students. I wasn't going to be on the front lines of sales. I'd be the expert that students could turn to when they had problems or questions. How bad could that be?

7.

In the beginning, working at Trump University was probably the best job I ever had. I traveled around the country, and it was the first time in my life that my job didn't feel like work.

I really loved it. I loved being the advisor and the person that the students came to for help.

Having craved attention all my life, now I was soaking in it. Every student wanted my time. I was the only person at Trump University who was an expert in real estate. They needed me, and I liked being needed. I even dared to imagine that given Michael Sexton's total lack of knowledge of real estate, I had a good shot at eventually taking over the education programs and running the entire organization.

Very quickly, though, the calls I received from students began to change in character. When a student called Trump University to complain about an unqualified instructor or mentor, the person receiving the call would occasionally transfer it to me. Fielding consumer complaints wasn't exactly in my job description, but I took the calls; and because of my expertise, I was often able to clarify real estate questions and satisfy the student. Soon, however, this meant that every complaint lodged against Trump University was transferred to me. With mounting frequency, I wasn't being asked to clarify some complex legal point made by an instructor at a workshop, or to help a student with the fine print of a deal: I was putting out fires and placating angry students.

I told Michael and Brad about the calls. Michael's response was that I should teach them. Brad told me that my goal should be preventing students from requesting refunds or, worse, filing a lawsuit. It seemed to me that he didn't really care about the academic quality of what we were providing or even whether the students were actually taught anything. "Fix it," he would say. "Fix it, and save the client."

"Save the client" was an interesting choice of words. It seemed what he really meant was that we got their money, and we should do what we could to keep it. The salespeople did their jobs. They got the money. It was our job to make sure we *kept* it. We had to say whatever we had to say to the student to make them forget about demanding a refund or suing us.

Increasingly, I was responsible for the failings of our lecturers and mentors. I had to close a huge gap between the expertise our students were *paying for* and the scandalous reality of what they were *actually getting*. I took a lot of pride in helping students, and I worked as hard as I could, but as the company grew and five thousand students were enrolled, it became impossible for me to interact with all of the angry ones. I was failing to fix them.

When fielding calls, I had two computers, and I multitasked between two different screens. On one computer I administrated the real estate game, and on the other I would look up real estate law and other facts.

One day, I got an incoming call from a student. Let's call him Sunil. He said, "I'm here at the Department of Records and Deeds trying to file documents, and they won't accept my paperwork."

"Okay," I said. "What are you trying to do?"

"I'm filing an affidavit to cloud a title," said Sunil, "and they won't take it."

This was a complicated real estate gambit that wasn't legal in every state. The term "cloud a title" refers to any irregularity in the chain of title of real property that would give a reasonable person pause before accepting a conveyance of title. A typical example is a memorandum of agreement—a legal affidavit—that states that you have an agreement with the owner of a property for the sale of that property. When properly notarized, this affidavit may be recorded in the county recorder's office. When you record the memorandum, it creates a "cloud" on the title that makes it difficult for another buyer to insure the title since it creates uncertainty about ownership interests in the property.

A list of states popped into my head and I noticed the 480 area code of his call. Phoenix, Arizona.

"You've made a mistake," I said. "What you're trying to do can't be done in the state of Arizona. It's illegal."

"But this is what our mentor told us to do," he said. "Wait, what?" I said. "Where did you learn this?"

"At the Trump University retreat in Scottsdale."

No, no, no, I thought. *This was not possible. There had to be a mistake.* As I clutched the phone the room seemed to spin around me. After taking a deep breath, I returned my attention to the student.

"Are you sure?" I asked. "Please tell me exactly what you were told. Who was your instructor?"

"A guy named Steve Goff."

Steve and Chris Goff were charismatic brothers and mentors at Trump University who traveled around the country hosting real estate retreats. Evidently, the Goff brothers were giving workshops whose core principles were illegal in some of the states where the retreats where held.

On one hand, why shouldn't you be able to play a middleman, brokering a deal? On the other hand, letting agents sign potentially hundreds of simultaneous purchase agreements without any money is ludicrous. It would be easy for a novice buyers and sellers to get taken advantage of this way. You can see why some states would want to limit this practice. Why should you be allowed to advertise a home for sale that you don't actually own?

In December 2007, David Lazarus, a reporter for the *Los Angeles Times*, ventured to the Pasadena Hilton to attend a free preview workshop hosted by Steve Goff. In his article entitled "Trump spins in foreclosure game," Lazarus related how Goff claimed that before being hired by Trump he had bought and sold three hundred houses. Goff quickly added that despite leading the event in Pasadena, he had never bought or sold a house in California. Lazarus asked Goff if he were a millionaire. He said no, admitting that he had been through bankruptcy and two divorces, and that he had his own home foreclosed upon.

According to AMI Newswire, in 2007—in the middle of his tenure with Trump University—Goff had indeed filed for bankruptcy. In a court in Texas, he cited at least $759,000 in debts against less than $20,000 in assets—not even enough to buy a Trump University Gold Elite Program. The value of his own real estate venture at the time was listed as zero dollars. Goff said that his bankruptcy had "nothing to do with real estate," implying that it was unfair to cite his bankruptcy when discussing his qualifications to teach real estate. Goff's bankruptcy listed his profession as real-estate consultant. It showed that a substantial portion of his debt involved his personal obligations on real-estate mortgages.

"I love helping people," Goff told Lazarus. "I'm very passionate about helping people achieve success."

As Lazarus soon discovered, the free preview turned out to be a two-hour infomercial for the workshop, which was being held that weekend at the Hilton Los Angeles North in Glendale.

During his hard-sell presentation, Goff repeatedly asserted that he didn't have enough time to fully explain particular real estate strategies, but that those who attended the workshop would hear many of Donald Trump's secrets. Lazarus walked away from the free preview with these precious nuggets of valuable information:

-Don't use your own money.

-Buy low and sell high.

-Set up a company so your deals won't be in your name.

Lazarus got the impression that the core of Trump's secret strategy— if you could call it that— was to find someone in financial trouble, make a low-ball offer for their home, and then sell that property to someone else at a higher price *before any money changed hands.*

"You do not have to *own* real estate to make money from it," Goff told the audience. "You just have to *control* it. You can control it with contracts."

There was nothing secret or revolutionary about any of this. Real estate speculators had been peddling such techniques for decades. You can buy a hundred self-help books that preach the same thing. The only added value was the Trump brand and his celebrity status, and the implication that his personal success and larger-than-life persona would, like medieval alchemy, turn run-down shacks into golden mansions.

"Why would you ever consider learning real estate from someone else?" Goff asked. "Trump is the best."

But the foreclosure market isn't for the novice, and it's very easy to lose your shirt on a deal that turns sour. Programs that push retirees and homemakers to gamble with their money represent the same sort of craziness that got us into the sub-prime quagmire in the first place.

However, in a perverse effort to appear socially responsible, Goff repeatedly stressed that the goal of investing in distressed properties wasn't to turn a fast buck. It was to uplift those who were less fortunate.

"We're here to help people get out of their situations," he said. "We're not here to take advantage of people."

Goff obfuscated the naked truth that such deals were predicated on taking advantage of someone in trouble. All you were doing is getting a higher price for a home than the owner would be able to get himself.

When the workshop finally ended, Lazarus reported that only four or five people signed up for the $1,495 workshop. The rest drifted out with perplexed looks on their faces, perhaps wondering why they'd never received the "priceless information" they'd been promised.

When the story by Larazus was published, Donald Trump threatened to sue the paper for libel.

Trump didn't sue, but he wrote an angry letter to the editor, Davan Maharaj. On December 13, 2007, the *Los Angeles Times* published it:

> To Mr. Maharaj:
>
> I am worth many billions of dollars, am building large scale developments all over the world, am considered by many to be, by far, the hottest name in real estate, and I have to read an article by a third-rate reporter in your newspaper that my "primary claim to fame" is hosting *The Apprentice*. Unlike many other people that make their money giving seminars, I made my money in real estate and, as your reporter should have known, I never filed for bankruptcy. In Los Angeles, for instance, I own (National 100%) one of the most successful and highly rated golf courses in the State of California, Trump in Palos Verdes. This golf and residential development, which fronts over a long stretch of the Pacific Ocean, was purchased for a mere fraction of its current worth—and that is what I teach at Trump University.
>
> When your reporter called me two weeks ago to ask questions about Trump University, a very successful though very small part of my business holdings, this reporter sounded like a real "wise-guy." Unfortunately, there are too many such people in the otherwise wonderful

profession of journalism. With people like this working for the *Los Angeles Times*, I now see why it is a newspaper in a tailspin—both from an advertising and circulatory standpoint. Try getting rid of your "bad apples" like this and I bet you will do a lot better—and by the way in last season's *Apprentice* the *Los Angeles Times* was all too anxious to partake in one of its episodes.

Sincerely,
Donald J. Trump
P.S. The picture, however, was great!

It's interesting that Trump claimed in the letter to have never filed for bankruptcy before. He must have forgotten about the string of Trump casino disasters in Atlantic City.

I returned to Sunil, my beleaguered student on the phone. He was in a bad situation. At a retreat in Scottsdale, he'd been given step-by-step instructions to do something that was illegal in Arizona. First, Sunil had negotiated and signed an illegal purchase agreement with a homeowner. Next, he visited the Department of Records and Deeds to file an affidavit that officially gave him first dibs on selling the property, like a right of first refusal. This protected him so that, for example, the seller and another buyer couldn't make a deal that excluded him. Filing such a document on the deed to a property did indeed constitute clouding the title. He got into trouble because the real estate broker who attended the open house blew the whistle on him because his name was not on the title.

He had paid five thousand dollars to Trump University to learn about real estate, he had done something illegal because that's what he had been taught, and then he had walked into the county deeds office with the very document that proved the illegal thing that he'd done. In Arizona, you can't market a property unless *you own it.* You'd be in violation of the contract and in violation for selling real estate without a license. Because this student had already signed an illegal purchase agreement, he could have been fined $10,000 and then sent to jail for a year.

That was an unforgivable mistake. If you're getting paid to teach real estate, you should know that laws vary from place to place. Any experienced real estate professional will know that looking up the local laws is easy to do and absolutely necessary. Teaching not just the wrong real estate method, but an actually illegal one, was beyond incompetence. It was an ethical violation. It was morally bankrupt.

"Are you still there?" Sunil said on the phone, startling me. I sat upright in my chair.

I apologized profusely to Sunil and assured him that we'd take care of the problem. I suggested that he hire a lawyer and break the illegal purchase agreement, even if he lost his escrow deposit. I suggested that this would be better than paying a fine and getting audited.

This wasn't the first or last fire that I had to put out at Trump University. It wasn't my job to correct the mentors, but I brought each issue to Brad Schneider, my direct supervisor, and to Trump University CEO Michael Sexton. "Send it to us in an email so we can address it," they would say.

So I sent them emails, a few at first, but then an increasing number. Eventually, I realized that many of the "mentors" were unqualified and should be audited. "You can't do this," I would say. "It's illegal in that state to do this. You need to contact all the mentors and stop them immediately."

To my knowledge, nothing ever came of these emails, because incidents kept happening at workshops and retreats, and they all could have been prevented. I didn't understand why nothing was being done. Students would call the hotline, and it became my sad duty to inform them that they couldn't do what the mentors told them that they could do. Of course, they were outraged. "What do you mean, I can't do that?" they would say. "This is what my mentor said I should do!"

At Trump University, I began to realize that lack of experience was a problem across the entire organization. It wasn't just that there were a few bad apples. Some of the mentors were selling their own real estate investments to students, even self-dealing to advance hidden agendas.

The stress mounted and mounted. I loved helping the students, but it was an overwhelming task—there were just too many of them who were truly angry and confused. My dream job was quickly becoming a nightmare.

8.

While I was trying to figure out how to reconcile my ambition with my increasing realization that many at Trump University were not behaving ethically, it seemed Donald Trump was continuing his strategy of relentlessly attaching his name to anything that could generate quick cash and elevate his stature.

He attached his name to a huge array of products and properties. Over the years, a typical consumer—let's call her Suzy—could jump from Trump product to Trump product like a retiree sampling the endless buffet at Golden Corral. Suzy could live in Trump Tower (or any number of other glitzy Trump addresses around the world); dine at Trump restaurants, including the Trump Grill and Trump Cafe; have a party catered by Trump Catering; and to cap off her evening enjoy dessert at the Trump Ice Cream Parlor before ordering a Trump Vodka Martini at Trump Bar. She would feel good knowing that, according to advertising for the product, Trump Vodka would "demand the same respect and inspire the same awe as the international legacy and brand of Donald Trump himself."

When planning a vacation she could search for a hotel on the short-lived GoTrump.com travel site while sipping her "Select By Trump" coffee drink, or if she needed a bigger boost she could pop open a bottle of an imported Trump energy drink, sold in the Israeli and Palestinian markets.

For her husband's birthday she could peruse the Donald J. Trump Signature Collection line of menswear, men's accessories, and watches, all manufactured in Asia, or if she wanted him to smell like money she could order a few bottles of either Donald Trump "The Fragrance" or SUCCESS by Donald Trump. Or perhaps he'd enjoy playing "The Game," Trump's 1989 board game given a 2004 re-release version tied to *The Apprentice*.

When thinking of re-doing her bedroom, Suzy could find the perfect accessory at Trump Home. She would be assured that, according to company, "every Trump Home masterpiece is handcrafted to perfection and made to order. Each magnificent piece of furniture is engineered using elite and exotic materials attained from around the world."

If she were creating a special event that needed fashion models, she could phone Trump Model Management. "With a name that symbolizes success," boasts the company's website, "the agency has risen to the top of the fashion market, producing models that appear on the pages of magazines such as *Vogue*, on designer runways, in advertising campaigns and blockbuster movies."

Tired from her Trump shopping spree, Suzy could quaff a refreshing bottle of "Trump Ice" bottled water, kick back with a copy of *Trump Magazine*, and enjoy some tasty gold-wrapped Trump chocolate. Suzy could join her friends or business colleagues for few rounds at her local Trump Golf course. His name is on fifteen golf courses in Scotland, Ireland, and across the Eastern Seaboard. For a night out, Suzy could enjoy a delicious Trump steak, either at home or at the Trump DJT steakhouse located in the Trump International Hotel in Las Vegas (but she should be careful, because in November of 2012, DJT was temporarily shut down after health inspectors found fifty-one health violations, and there is no Trump brand anti-diarrheal medication, though perhaps there should be).

If Suzy wanted to visit relatives in Boston, she could hop on the Trump shuttle, the former Eastern Airlines shuttle. It is worth mentioning that this particular toy of Trump's quickly became a pointless disaster. Trump didn't know anything about the economics of the airline business. On aging airplanes that were worth about $4 million each, Trump spent about $1 million apiece to turn them into little flying palaces dedicated to Donald Trump.

He had a "T" emblazoned on the tail of each plane as big as possible. A giant TRUMP was painted on the side. Inside, the wood paneling was made of bird's eye maple. The burgundy carpet was the most plush in the business, but it was too thick: the center panel had to be ripped up after flight attendants struggled to push drink carts down the aisle.

The in-flight magazines featured Trump on the cover. Even the labels on the wet-naps had "Trump Shuttle" printed on them. New seat belt buckles were made of chrome. In the lavatories, Trump ordered sinks of faux pink marble. The lights installed were bright makeup lights, not the dim fluorescents that most planes had.

Trump wanted all the flight attendants to wear necklaces with costume pearls. Trump designed new uniforms for them that showed ample cleavage, and only after the women complained was the design changed.

It became the usual story: expenses were out of control, and over an eighteen-month period, the Trump Shuttle had lost $128 million. Did Trump care? Not a bit. According to news reports at the time, Trump was no longer responsible for the $245 million in loans still left to pay on the Trump Shuttle.

In addition, out of the $135 million that Trump had personally guaranteed, at least $100 million was forgiven by the banks. Trump told the Boston Globe, "I got out at a good time. I walked away saying, 'I'm smart.' It's good to get great financing. . . . I felt successful. The market had crashed. I didn't lose anything. It was a good thing."

Trump put his name on just about anything that could add to his wealth, either through actual sales or by using other people's money and then walking away when the deal went south. It surprised me that Trump never introduced a line of Trump toilet paper, gold-trimmed for prestige and double-quilted for exceptional softness. It would have been a big seller, I'm sure.

But you can bet that he would have convinced someone else to put up the money.

In April 2006, Donald Trump hosted a glitzy event at Trump Tower to publicly introduce Trump Mortgage LLC, his new firm that specialized in brokering residential and commercial real estate loans. He dedicated a floor of 40 Wall Street to the business, which had been operating quietly since late 2005. Trump's picture appeared atop the company website with the instruction, "Talk to My Mortgage Professionals Now!"

"If you had told me we would have had this many people for a friggin' mortgage company opening—give me a break," said Donald Trump, speaking to several hundred people crammed into a lower level space at Trump Tower. It's not typical that a mortgage company launch at eleven o'clock in the morning would be a media circus. But such is the way of life in the world of Donald J. Trump.

Trump was joined by E.J. Ridings, the new company's president and CEO, and his son Donald Trump Jr., who is also involved in the project. Sadly, Ivanka—who was scheduled to attend and whom the press especially wanted to see—didn't show up.

"When Don and I struck the deal," crowed Trump, "We said, 'We'll have a news conference.' What we didn't expect was *Extra!*, *Access Hollywood, Entertainment Tonight*, and some of the other folks up here. Take a look—there's my friend Lois Weiss from the *New York Post*."

"The business they're doing is unbelievable," he continued, referring to the new mortgage company. "Literally, we signed the lease a few months ago, and they are going to take an additional floor."

To appease the hungry audience, as well as the startled tourists riding up and down the escalator overhead, snapping photos on cell phones, Trump delivered his famous catch phrase. He told E.J. Ridings that he needed to make sure the company was keeping up with the current pace, or else... "E.J., you're fired!"

Everybody had a good laugh, and Trump's newest self-titled company was officially launched. A mortgage firm is essentially a middleman between lenders and homeowners. The lenders, usually banks, get connected to millions of homeowners through the work of mortgage brokers, who "broker" the deals.

To operate, a mortgage firm needs a portfolio lending license and a banker's license. Mortgage brokers will work with any bank that they're approved to work with. Often they'll make the banks compete and choose the one with the best terms. They'll also work with other mortgage companies, outsourcing the loan applications process. Then the loan officer and the mortgage broker charge a fee of two or three percent. This money can be paid up front by the homeowner or added to the loan amount, to be paid off over time.

Donald Trump went on CNBC and announced, "I think it's a great time to start a mortgage company . . . The real estate market is going to be very strong for a long time to come . . . We're going to have a great company. It's Trump Mortgage and trumpmortgage. com. And it's going to be a terrific company."

And so Trump Mortgage was born, joining the ranks of other illustrious Trump ventures including Trump steaks, *Trump Magazine*, and Trump water.

Chief executive officer E.J. Ridings had been introduced to Donald Trump by his son, Donald Trump, Jr. Ridings boasted in interviews that the new company "would own New York" and then expand to all fifty states, offering residential and commercial mortgages.

"Trump Mortgage is going to take better care of people than anyone in the mortgage industry ever has," Trump said at the time. Ridings agreed. "The housing boom has attracted a variety of people into this business, not all of them honest," he told *Money Magazine* in September. "I really believe that the public needs and wants a safe place to get a mortgage."

Trump Mortgage manager Jan Scheck, who left the company after one year, later told the *Washington Post* that he recalled being awed as he stood alongside Trump at the opening news conference at Trump Tower in 2006. "I told myself this was an awesome opportunity with somebody who was a god in the real estate industry. People were buying Trump ties . . . You have to remember, this is the peak of his popularity. Everybody wanted to be Donald Trump. Donald was putting his name on buildings all over the country. I thought this was going to be an awesome opportunity."

Scheck said that the floor devoted to Trump Mortgage was divided into two units. One side was an upscale residential and commercial mortgage business, which Scheck ran. The other side was known internally as the "boiler room," where employees often made cold calls to people seeking to refinance or originate loans, many of them "sub-prime," meaning the borrowers had poor credit histories.

The company, which was authorized to do business in fifteen states, talked a good game. "Whether people need a fifty-thousand-dollar line of credit or a three-million-dollar mortgage, whether it's residential or commercial, whether they have perfect credit or credit in need of repair, they all deserve the same service," Ridings told *Multi-Housing News*. The Trump Mortgage website—which you can still access at webarchive.org—described the CEO in glowing terms:

E.J. Ridings is one of the most accomplished professionals in the New York City mortgage arena. He brings to Trump Mortgage over fifteen years' experience in the financial industry, and a comprehensive, hands-on knowledge of the mortgage and commercial/residential lending business. From the very beginning, Ridings demonstrated a rare talent for launching successful business ventures. He founded his first company shortly after graduating from college with a business degree, and launched his second start-up a mere six years later. With Ridings' keen financial acumen and exceptional management skills, both of his organizations achieved immediate, sustained success and rapid growth.

Ridings' desire to possess an even broader under-standing of the financial world led him to a variety of positions within the financial community. He has been a highly-successful independent stock trader, a top executive for one of the most prestigious investment banks on Wall Street, and an established leader at one of New York City's top boutique mortgage firms. A born entrepreneur, Ridings began to envision starting up a new mortgage company, one that would ultimately be an industry leader.

In fact, Ridings was an unlikely candidate for being described as a "top professional on Wall Street." Once on the radar screens of financial reporters, Trump Mortgage quickly ran into bad publicity. The press discovered that E.J. Ridings was like a guy trying to swim in the Olympics who had barely gotten out of the kiddie pool. In December 2006, *Money* published a damning exposé of the Trump Mortgage CEO. According to documents from the New York State Attorney General's office, Ridings worked at Morgan Stanley's bro-kerage subsidiary Dean Witter Reynolds in the fall of 1998 for less than three months. During that time, he was a registered broker for *six days* before leaving the firm.

Trump Mortgage claimed that Ridings was an "established leader" at one of New York's leading mortgage boutiques. But according to former colleagues, Ridings was a relatively minor player at the mortgage boutique GuardHill Financial, where he worked from June 2003 to April 2005.

The Trump Mortgage bio also boasted that Ridings had fifteen years of experience in the financial industry. But according to documents obtained by *Money* from the New York State Banking Department, Ridings's first job in the financial services industry was his brief time as a broker at Morgan Stanley in late 1998. The documents also said he was a day trader for two years and worked at subprime lending firm Equity Funding for one year before joining GuardHill. Ridings's actual professional experience was not in mortgages but in the nutritional supplement business. In the mid-1990s, he founded a company that sold a variety of vitamins and health drinks. Before that, he owned a cleaning service.

Why did Donald Trump Jr. take an ordinary businessman and introduce him to his billionaire father, and then promote him as a good choice to head a New York mortgage company which was promising first-year sales of $3 billion? Donald Trump Jr. never offered an explanation.

Despite Trump's glowing comments about the good timing for the venture, when Trump Mortgage was launched, the real estate market was already headed into the dumpster. The mortgage market had peaked in 2003, when interest rates hit forty-year lows, and residential sales topped out in 2005. The company was building a business in the subprime arena just as that market was collapsing.

Writing mortgages is a complex business, and to launch a successful mortgage company—especially in New York City—you need the very best mortgage brokers. One big problem was that the company failed to attract and retain these top mortgage brokers. At least six residential mortgage professionals left the firm within a year, including Scheck and Craig Lane, who had been hired to run the company's Florida operations.

Trump Mortgage quickly fell short of Ridings' rosy forecasts. At the time of the company's launch, Ridings predicted the company would complete three billion dollars in loans in 2006, much of it in residential lending. Just a few months later, Ridings furiously back-pedaled, saying, "Trump Mortgage anticipated doing close to one billion dollars in residential mortgages, but that figure may not be reached by the end of this year."

As Trump Mortgage slowly crumbled under its bad management, Michael Sexton called me and said, "Since you're the mortgage guy, why don't you go up and fix Trump Mortgage?" He asked me to take a look at it, to see what I thought about it.

Trump Mortgage was ensconced at 40 Wall Street, a few floors above us. I set up a meeting with the top guys at Trump Mortgage, and when I arrived I could not believe the look of these financiers. They looked like mobsters. One character with black, greased-back hair wore a sharkskin suit, skinny tie, and shiny black alligator shoes.

I said, "Hi, I'm Steve from downstairs at Trump U. Michael Sexton asked me to come up to learn about Trump Mortgage and speak with you guys briefly. We heard you're having some problems getting mortgages into the system and trying to write mortgages." Then I introduced myself as a longtime owner of a mortgage company who could help.

While they weren't rude, their vibe was cool. They did not seem to want my advice. They were older, in their forties and fifties, and treated me like a lightweight. I could sense them rolling their eyes and thinking, "Here's a hotshot kid coming in, trying to tell us what to do with our company."

I was shocked to learn that they were running loans through private money. They would borrow private money from other companies, write mortgages, and not sell off the paper. They were making loans without having a line of credit from a legitimate bank. It appeared that they were doing subprime loans.

Trump Mortgage was also charging too much in fees. There are limits under the law to how much you can charge and it seemed to me they went beyond those limits. Lenders such as Fannie Mae, Freddie Mac, the VA, and the FHA, have guidelines that can run to more than a thousand pages. Mortgage brokers have to know and follow those guidelines and legal regulations.

For example, a mortgage writer must verify the homeowner's assets by doing an appraisal of the home. They must ask for the borrower's job history, tax returns, and several other documents. Trump Mortgage wasn't verifying these loans. They were just giving them out like candy to earn the fees. I would guess that some ninety percent of the borrowers defaulted because they just couldn't afford the loan terms and should never have been offered a mortgage.

The employees were legal mortgage brokers, but, like Trump University, they seemed very unethical. The entire company didn't seem right to me. Trump Mortgage was never solvent, even from the very beginning. I advised Michael to close the organization immediately. Get out while you can and take Trump's name off of it immediately, I said.

Within eighteen months after its gala launch at Trump Tower, as the real estate meltdown became a boiling cauldron of despair, Trump Mortgage closed, leaving bills unpaid, a spotty sales record that fell short of Trump's lofty predictions, and at least one lawsuit by a former broker who alleged she was stiffed on a commission. Jennifer McGovern worked in what she described as the boutique part of the business, where people who were housed in their own offices dealt with high-end real estate agents and attorneys. She told *Bloomberg Markets* that she recalled Trump coming into the mortgage office and giving pep talks to employees. She didn't know that around the same time he was also rooting for the housing collapse so that he could buy property cheaply.

In early 2007, McGovern sued Trump Mortgage. She had brokered a $26.5 million commercial loan that should have given her a $238,000 payment, she said. Trump Mortgage told her to accept a $10,000 commission instead. When she refused, she said Ridings fired her on the spot.

"Why would I ever agree to $10,000 when I know we are making all this money from it and I have an employment contract?" she said. In 2009, McGovern won a court judgment awarding her a payout close to $300,000. But by then, the company had no assets, no office, and no phone number.

Trump distanced himself from the ugly death of Trump Mortgage, saying that he had not been involved in the company's management and that its executives had performed poorly. Not surprisingly, he blamed the people he had personally hired to run the company. "We weren't happy with them and we terminated them based on the fact they were not doing what they said they were going to do," he told the *Real Deal*, a New York trade publication, in September 2007.

Of all of Trump's ventures outside his core real estate business—the airline, the steaks, the vodka, the magazine, the board game, the travel website—it was this one, perhaps more than any other, that clashed with the image of the financial guru that he had brashly cultivated. Not only did the episode expose Trump's shoddy rush into a market on the verge of collapse, but his failure happened in an industry that should have been his forte—real estate. As for where the money went, the firm collected fees for being a middleman, or intermediary, between borrowers and banks. The company didn't do any actual lending, making it hard to uncover documents and data on the number of loans it handled.

To keep his hand in the industry, Trump then licensed his name to First Meridian Mortgage.

David Brecher was tapped to run the firm, which became known as Trump Financial. At the time, *Crain's* reported that Trump Financial would be the preferred lender on Trump development projects. In most of the dozen states where it operated, First Meridian would operate as Trump Financial. It would stay First Meridian in some of the markets in which it still had high name recognition, such as in Brooklyn.

"The Trump name opens doors and gets people to call back," said Brecher, adding that his company would carve out a niche at the high end of the market. After a few years, Trump Financial shut down, just like Trump Mortgage.

9.

The Trump Mortgage meltdown made me think. The problem with Trump Mortgage wasn't lazy executives or a few bad apples, like Trump suggested. It was the entire execution of the company. And it wasn't an accidental flaw. From the start, the organization was structured to be shoddy. The company's management didn't want to fix Trump Mortgage. They wanted to take the money and run. It was a wake-up call for me.

An upcoming Trump University workshop was being held in New York, where I was based. I decided to go to the hotel to see one of these speakers who was earning $25,000 to speak for a couple of days. I thought wow, *they can speak for six hours-plus and get $25,000? I want that job!*

The presenter was James A. Harris. The seats quickly filled inside the ballroom at the Trump International Hotel and Tower. The place was decorated with impressive-looking Trump University signage. At the front of the room, Donald Trump stared down from two big posters. The Trump University staff were attired in expensive suits and had fresh haircuts. They looked like perfect models of Young Wealth.

From my seat in the back of the room, I watched as the prospects were each equipped with a Trump brand pad and pen. After they had been thoroughly warned against using cell phones to make recordings, the lights dimmed and James Harris jogged to the front of the room. He wore a Tommy Bahama shirt and had thin, black-framed glasses. His shoes and hair looked sleek and expensive. On his wrist was a big gold watch.

As he prowled the area in front of the room like a hungry tiger, Harris said into his microphone, "How are you all doing tonight?"

The response was timid, which he found unacceptable. "C'mon, guys!" he shouted.

"Good!" everyone responded, this time with more gusto.

Harris began the show by introducing himself. The goal was to make the audience feel like they knew him personally. It's a lot easier to hand over your kid's college tuition money to a guy who you think is your trusted friend rather than a stranger that you just met at a hotel. It did not take me long to realize that everything that came out of the man's mouth was a lie, and that many of his gullible students believed that it was gospel.

Like a master thespian, Harris told the hushed and attentive audience that his father had left home when he was a boy and that his mother was addicted to drugs. By the time he was nineteen he was sleeping in New York City subway tunnels, with no future and no hope.

Then an unnamed mentor taught him how to sell real estate. This had changed his life. In no time, said Harris, he "became one of the top twelve producing brokers" in Manhattan. He had pulled himself up and gotten fabulously wealthy. He no longer slept among vermin, but now lived in a luxurious gated community in Buford, Georgia, with his wife and two sons. Now he wanted to help everyone in the room to get wealthy too.

During his inspiring rags-to-riches story, Harris had omitted some juicy details. Despite being the top "instructor" at an institution that billed itself as a university, he didn't have a background in education or even a college degree. When he was hired in 2008, he had a felony conviction for ramming into someone's truck with his own truck eight years earlier. And according to 2011 divorce filings in Gwinnett County, Georgia, Harris had threatened to kill his ex-wife and tried to have her Range Rover repossessed the day after she filed a restraining order against him. Harris was so volatile, according to court records, that his children's school went on lockdown one day when he picked up his kids. Officials now required that custody exchanges with his wife occur off school property.

Trump University did run a background check on Harris, but the investigators did not flag his criminal record. They were also apparently not able to verify whether he graduated from high school, though Harris later told CNN that he did graduate. The report didn't uncover any real estate experience either, according to court records. There is no evidence that James Harris ever held a real estate license.

"Write this down," Harris told his audience. "Your license plate when I'm done with you is going to say PAID FOR. Got that?"

I quickly understood that the hapless Preview attendees were getting only the merest glimpse of "the real estate secrets of Donald Trump." Harris used a simple but effective sleight of hand. He'd mention a subject, like closing costs or title searches, and then quickly say, "We'll talk about that more later."

But heck, what did these poor suckers expect at a free preview? You want the wealth-building secrets of The Donald? Then you'd better get out your checkbook, because he ain't giving them away for free! Harris also omitted that he was being paid a hefty commission for every sale that he made.

As far as I could tell, the wisdom dispensed that night by James Harris and Trump University was about on par with the information that Steve Goff had given to reporter David Lazarus:

— Buy low, sell high

— Use other people's money to do your deals.

— Don't do business in your own name, or you'll lose your shirt if you ever have to file for bankruptcy protection. (Donald Trump knew a lot about bankruptcy).

— Find people facing foreclosure, make them a low offer, and then sell for more before any money changes hands.

I saw at least one big legal problem with what Harris was teaching: he didn't seem to know anything about the Home Equity Theft Prevention Act (HETPA), which was a New York State law that had passed on July 26, 2006. The law discloses information to homeowners of residential property in order to help them make careful decisions when approached by persons seeking a sale or transfer of the homeowner's property, particularly when homeowners are in default on their mortgage payments or the property is in foreclosure. The law generally applies to the sale of a home in foreclosure to a buyer who wants to purchase the home as an investment.

The law is very strict. The equity purchaser is prohibited from making any contract that takes unconscionable advantage of the equitable seller. It makes "flipping" an underwater home extremely difficult. For example, the law says that an equity purchaser shall make no false or misleading statements regarding: the value of the property, the amount of proceeds the equity seller will receive after a foreclosure sale, the timing of the judicial foreclosure process, any contract term, the equity seller's rights and obligations, or the nature of any document which the equity purchaser induces the equity seller to sign. The law also forbids the equity purchaser from making any other false or misleading statements concerning the sale of the property or concerning a reconveyance arrangement.

If a sale is protected by the law, and the buyer fails to fulfill any of the requirements of the law, the seller may be able to void or legally cancel the contract they have with the buyer, even after it has been signed. Likewise, a sale may be declared void. The seller may also be able to sue the buyer to recover any damages. It was precisely ignorance of this law that led to Trump University eventually being kicked out of several states including Florida, Arizona, and Texas.

"Are you *with* me?" bellowed Harris.

Most of the people in the audience nodded meekly.

"Are you with me, class?" he shouted again. "Give me a big 'yes!'"

"Yes!" the audience replied.

"Are the markets gonna turn in Florida?" he asked.

"Yes!"

"Are you with me?"

"Yes!"

An Internet advertisement appeared on the big screen. The text read, "Need to sell fast? We buy your house for cash! Top prices paid!"

"Guys," Harris said, "do you want to use my ads?" "Yeah!" somebody yelled back.

"What do you say?" demanded Harris. "Please!"

"Sure," said Harris. "All you have to do is ask."

I could feel the people in the room getting soft. Harris was converting them. Harris had a powerful incentive to sell. As with all the other presenters at the free Preview or the $1,495 workshops, Harris was paid a hefty twenty-five percent of whatever upsell tickets he managed to unload. Harris's upsell rate was so good that Trump University executives distributed a transcript of one of his sessions so that others could learn his secrets, especially from the crucial elements of his unscripted Q&A at the end, where the master pitchman closed his sales.

Among the highlights of Harris's winning presentation was his promise that Trump "only wants to leave a legacy. He does not need your fifteen hundred dollars. He did not have to start this university. He does not need the money. He does not get a dime of it. Does everyone understand this? Please say 'yes.' He does not need the money."

As far as I could tell, the only real information the attendees received at the preview was how to negotiate with their credit card company for a higher line of credit. Harris coached them on how to fudge their income and assets, and how to inform the credit agent that it was "too much trouble" to put together the paperwork to back up their desperate need for more credit. The gambit was based on the premise that a higher line of credit would be necessary when it came time to buy up all those bargain properties, the locations of which would be revealed to the student in the special three-day workshop for the low, low price of $1,495.

To the retiree sitting in the audience who was looking for a new career, or to the guy who was between jobs and disillusioned about his prospects, or to the woman who had heard about people making money flipping houses and believed in Donald Trump's gospel of success, $1,495 may have seemed like a lot of money. But they had already come all this way to the free Preview. They had gotten all dressed up in their Sunday best and were perhaps embarrassed to admit to the sleek Trump salespeople that they couldn't afford the price, or—even worse!—were *too meek* to take the plunge. In the world of Donald Trump, there is no sin greater than timidity. Trump recognizes only winners and losers, and people who are indecisive or circumspect are *losers*.

In the grand scheme of things, what was a measly $1,495? It wasn't that much money, because the prospect would receive the priceless wisdom that Donald Trump had earned over the course of forty years building his vast empire. Indeed, compared to what the prospect owed on their mortgage, it was a drop in the bucket. If someone was afraid to pony up a mere $1,495—heck, Donald Trump, in his infinite generosity, was probably *losing* money on the course—then they deserved to live the pathetic life of a timid mouse.

Harris, with his gold watch and smooth delivery, told each of the prospects that *you*—yes, you, the retired janitor or suburban soccer mom—were truly a *gifted salesperson*. You had what it took— if only you listened to your inner lion.

As the presentation neared its conclusion, Harris, mopping his brow and sipping from an Evian bottle, launched into his closing gambit. He said that he had taught the attendees some good ways to make money, but there was *so much more to learn!* He said Trump University was hosting a very special three-day workshop in two weeks. There, and only there, would the most powerful secrets be revealed to those individuals who were truly motivated to improve their lives. The price was a mere $1,495.

"There are three groups of people," he proclaimed. "People who *make* things happen, people who *wait* for things to happen, and people who wonder, '*What happened?*' Which one are you?"

Harris even hinted at the prospect of Donald Trump himself attending the three-day workshop, saying, with a wink and a nod because *he wasn't supposed to reveal this*, that "Mr. Trump will be in town that weekend," and that he "often drops by" to meet his new pupils. Of course, Harris was very careful not to actually *say* Donald Trump would be at the workshop, because in reality Trump had no intention of wasting his time schmoozing with the suckers at his workshops. But the message to the starry-eyed prospects was delivered, loud and clear.

It was like hearing that if you went to the Ringo Starr concert there was a good chance that Paul McCartney would bound onstage to join him for a few Beatles numbers (to be fair to these ex-Beatles, the chances of Paul singing a few tunes with Ringo were better than Trump showing up at one of his own workshops). Harris flashed a picture on the big screen of himself. He was standing in his bathrobe between a Hummer and a Mercedes.

"I told you I work in my bathrobe," he said.

The next shot was of him and two young boys. He got serious. "This is why I work," he said, looking like he was about to burst into tears. "Don't do this for yourself. Do it for your kids. Do it for somebody else." Harris had an endless supply of slogans and catch phrases.

"The only reason I'm up here is because I have a little more confidence than you," he told the prospects. "But I can *give* you confidence. I can give you that shot in the shoulder you need."

And then, "There are gonna-bes and wanna-bes. And I want to talk to the gonna-bes when we're done." And then—incorrectly, brazenly—he said, "It's a tax write-off. So you'll get it back."

As the presentation reached its climax, I realized that James Harris was a pretty slick dude. In my mind, his pitch to the prospects in front of him consisted of a simple progression based on rock-solid logic:

1. You came here tonight because you want to improve your life.
2. I have shown you, in clear terms, how you can improve your life.
3. Therefore, you have *no reason* to turn away. Lack of money is not a reason. Fear is not a reason. Your current crummy life is not a reason.
4. If you want to feel like a *loser*, then go home. If you want to feel like a *winner*, then step up and sign on the dotted line. The money will come back to you in a flood.

In the final moments, he told those who wanted to get rich to head for the sign-up tables in the back. Those who were fearful or timid?

Well, they should just leave. Many people made for the door. But a sizable number went to the tables in the back. It looked to me like a pretty impressive conversion rate.

At the tables, the prospects were met by Trump employees who had been trained with the *Trump University Sales Play Book*. During this final critical stage of the sales process, it was the responsibility of the Trump salespeople to cheerfully overcome any lingering doubts the prospects had. This last step had been carefully planned in advance, and the *Play Book* set forth precise responses to every possible objection that prospects might offer. Here are just two of them, quoted directly from the *Play Book*:

Objection: "That's a lot of money."
Response: "That's a lot of money! Really? Most people look at this and are so excited that it's only that amount with everything we include. However, let's figure it out for you right now. What are your expenses every month? $3,000? OK, you are making $6,000 a month. What are your interest rates on your credit cards? Twelve percent. Perfect." (Take the percentage rate and divide it by twelve months that will give you the percent per month that they are charged. Then, take the amount that they are spending and divide it by their percentage per month.) "I see that your percentage rate per month is one percent. Let's take that number and see what your monthly payment will be. You will be paying $350 per month in interest and plus a little bit in minimum, so let's say you will have a payment on your credit card of around $600 dollars. Now that I showed you how you can afford it, I will not let you say 'no.' I just figured out how you

can have a Trump certified mentor fit into your budget for less than $600 per month. Let's get you a Mentor and get you to a whole new level of thinking and investing."

Objection: "I don't want to go into debt."

Response: "Every single company goes into debt when they are first starting out. *Every single business!* The profits pay off the debt and before you know it, your new real-estate business will start making amazing returns. Is it worth a small investment to own your own company, finally be your own boss, and keep all the profits that you make! If you're willing to work as hard for yourself as you have been for your boss I don't see you ever looking back. Imagine having the freedom to pick up kids from school, never miss another recital or sports game again because you made the decision to not allow fear and comfort zones to hold you back anymore in life. Let's get you a Mentor and get you to a whole new level of thinking and investing."

I watched as the prospects got out their credit cards and the smiling Trump employees took the cards and ran the charges. The Trump employees could not have been nicer or sounded more sincere. If you had walked in off the street and looked at the scene with no knowledge of the context, you would have thought that millionaires were being made that night.

Aside from the blatantly fact-free content of Harris' pitch, he was a spectacular salesman.

Like a hustling Houdini, the guy could slip your watch off your wrist and then sell it back to you. He was good enough to flout the

Trump *Play Book*. Trump University speakers were supposed to follow a three-stage sales process over the three days of the workshop. The first day was a "soft sell," which could be defined as inviting the attendee to buy one of the Elite packages. The second day was a "medium sell," where you apply a little more pressure and emphasize the life-changing possibilities of the program, though technically salespeople were forbidden to make specific performance claims, such as "If you attend this training, you will be able to make ten thousand dollars within the next sixty days." The third day was the "hard sell," where the salesperson twisted the emotional thumbscrews and tried to make the attendees feel like either a) courageous winners if they joined up with Trump, or b) pathetic losers if they didn't.

James Harris was so good at mesmerizing his audience that on a good first day he could go from soft sell to medium and all the way to hard. Every speaker was required to convert twenty-five percent of his or her audience into sales. So if you had two hundred paying attendees, you needed to sell a package to fifty of them. By lunchtime on the first day, Harris would be pressing with his hard sell, and when the group came back from their break he'd close them. By the end of the day he'd have his fifty people—and then some—lined up with their credit cards at the staff tables at the back of the room. On the second and third days, you could find him smoking a cigar in the bar while a second-stringer slogged through the presentation in the ballroom. James Harris had sold these people the dream—but who was going to make it come true?

10.

While James Harris and many other hardcore salespeople charged ahead with the Trump University business plan of grabbing money first and answering questions later, a few of the top stars actually felt conflicted and decided to leave the company. One of them was Ronald Schnackenberg, who had served as a sales manager at the Trump Organization from October 2006 through May 2007. He worked out of 40 Wall Street, selling Trump University programs to consumers who called to inquire and also selling programs at live events.

"I resigned from my position in May 2007 because I believe that Trump University was engaging in misleading, fraudulent and dishonest conduct," said Schnackenberg. "I found it particularly offensive that, while Trump University claimed it wanted to help consumers make money in real estate, in fact Trump University was only interested in selling every person the most expensive seminars they possibly could."

He said he believed it was a "fraudulent scheme and that it preyed on the elderly and uneducated to separate them from their money." In a sworn statement released in June 2016, Schnackenberg told the story of a couple he had talked to the month before he quit. The Moores didn't have enough money to pay the $34,995 fee for the Trump Gold Elite package. "I did not feel it was an appropriate program for them because of their precarious financial condition," he stated. "Trump University reprimanded me for not trying harder to sell the program to this couple." Schnackenberg said that salesman Tad Lignell talked the Moores into using the husband's disability income and a home equity loan to pay for the Trump Gold Elite package. Schnackenberg also questioned the qualifications of the instructors, recalling one whose background was in jewelry making rather than real estate.

"I believe most of the instructors, mentors, and coaches had very little or no experience in the real estate techniques they were teaching," he said. "I received complaints from Trump University students about this. . . . In my experience, virtually all students who purchased a Trump University seminar were dissatisfied with the program they purchased. To my knowledge, not a single consumer who paid for a Trump University seminar program went on to successfully invest in real estate based upon the techniques they were taught."

He added, "I never once saw Donald Trump at [the] Trump University [offices]. In seven months I worked at Trump University, I did not see him once."

Even though others were already leaving Trump University, I made the decision to keep going to work and to do my best to keep up with the relentless stream of phone calls from unhappy students. I could at least offer them real information, even if no one else could. Under the circumstances, it was the best thing for me to do.

One day, I found myself thrust into the world of Presidential politics. On November 6, 2008, at eight o'clock in the evening, two days after Barack Obama's election as America's first African American president, Sexton asked me to do a webcast. The thrust of it was to comment on the new President in an unfavorable light.

I was puzzled. Trump had just publicly praised the new President. The day after the election, he had appeared with Greta Van Susteren on Fox's "On the Record." She had asked him, "We have a President-elect, President-elect Obama, facing an incredible challenge with this economy. I realize he doesn't take office until sometime in January, but what should he be doing right now?"

"First of all," replied Trump, "This is a hell of a way for him to celebrate his first day with this massive, almost crash of the stock market. So this is one hell of a welcoming—it's a welcome to the President, Mr. President. And it's pretty sad. But what he's got to do, he's got to get the banks to liquefy the system. There's no money in the system, everybody is hoarding their money. The government is giving billions and billions of dollars to the banks and they are using it to buy other banks. I guess they are using it to clean up the balance sheet? But they are using it to loan to people to go out and do deals and build buildings and build housing, or for people to just go out and buy housing."

"The new president-elect," she pressed him a few minutes later. "What are your thoughts? Pretty exciting, it's always exciting when we have a change of power, a transition, but what are your thoughts?"

"It's very exciting we have a new president," replied Trump. "It would have been nice if he ended with a five-hundred-point up instead of down. It's certainly very exciting. His speech was great last night. I thought it was inspiring in every way. And, hopefully he's going to do a great job. But the way I look at it, he cannot do worse than Bush."

He didn't talk about Obama's birth certificate. The idea that Obama had been born in Kenya had been suggested six months earlier, during the Democratic Party primary, by a volunteer in the Hillary Clinton campaign. While Clinton's staff quickly rejected it, the theme had been enthusiastically embraced by little-known right-wing fringe figures like Orly Taitz and Philip Berg, and by the pundit Jerome Corsi. The false allegations claimed that Obama was a Muslim, that he had attended a "radical madrassa" in Indonesia, that he had been sworn into the U.S. Senate using the Koran, and that he had been born in Kenya and flown to Hawaii as an infant.

On June 13, 2008, to combat the persistent "birtherism" attacks, the Obama campaign launched FightTheSmears.com. One page debunked the birther conspiracy with the "Certificate of Live Birth" computer printout version of Obama's birth certificate, which is what the government in Hawaii sends you if you request a new copy. Even though it was his valid birth certificate for all legal purposes, this release served to only stoke the fires of the conspiracy theorists because it was not the original from 1961. These theories persisted even after Hawaiian government officials spoke of seeing and authenticating the original.

In November 2008 I had no particular reason to think that Donald Trump was interested in the birther lies, and he had just made positive—or at least non-negative—comments about Barack Obama to Greta Van Susteren. But Sexton wanted to make sure the webcast was not complimentary to the new president.

Sexton and Highbloom also made a startling request. They told several senior executives, including me, that Mr. Trump wanted to obtain a copy of Barack Obama's birth certificate, and had made a public announcement of this. They stated he was willing to pay as much as one hundred and fifty thousand dollars.

I actually took the challenge, and, through the efforts of an ex-student of mine and a friend of a friend of a friend, I procured a copy of Barack Obama's birth certificate. I made copies of it and we passed them around the office, and we joked about it.

So what was the outcome? Was Donald Trump told about my successful mission? If he was, he chose to ignore it. I never saw the prize money! Three years later, on February 10, 2011, when he was first considering a run for the presidency, Trump publicly embraced the birther conspiracy with a deliberately vague comment at the Conservative Political Action Conference: "Our current president came out of nowhere. Came out of nowhere. In fact, I'll go a step further: the people that went to school with him, they never saw him, they don't know who he is. It's crazy."

The next month Trump went on "The View." When he was asked if he believed President Obama had been born in the United States, he responded, "Why doesn't he show his birth certificate? And you know what? I wish he would... Nobody from those early years remembers him... There's something on that birth certificate he doesn't like."

Trump also said repeatedly that he had sent a team of investigators to Hawaii to unearth information about the president's birth records. "They cannot believe what they are finding," he said.

Even after Obama's long-form birth certificate was released on April 27, Trump continued to express doubts about its authenticity.

Consider the testimony of Jeff Lichter, a member of the so-called Surprise Tea Party Patriots (STPP) who asked Joe Arpaio, the flamboyant sheriff of Maricopa County, Arizona, to investigate the birth certificate. As the *Arizona Republic* reported, during a presentation to an STPP group, Lichter said that when he and two state lawmakers traveled to New York in April 2011 and met with Trump in Trump Tower, the businessman told them he anticipated Obama would be releasing a fake birth certificate.

"My sources in D.C. are telling me there is going to be a fake birth certificate," Lichter quoted Trump as saying.

In a letter dated August 20, 2011, the STPP asked Arpaio to investigate Obama's birth certificate. Arpaio had received the letter three days after Jerome Corsi, an author and reporter for *World Net Daily*, spoke to an STPP gathering about his doubts on Obama's birth records. The group gathered over two hundred signatures on a petition asking Arpaio to investigate whether Obama's birth certificate was a forgery.

The issue simmered over the years and then flared up again during the 2016 presidential campaign. Then, at a news conference on Friday, September 16, 2016, Donald Trump abruptly announced, "President Barack Obama was born in the United States. Period."

Trump's public abandonment of the issue didn't deter Sheriff Joe Arpaio, who continued to make statements asserting his belief that the birth certificate was a forgery. On September 20, Arpaio told an STPP group, "I'm not going to give up, and we're looking into it. I don't know how it's going to turn out." For Arpaio, the statement by Donald Trump that Obama was born in this country had no weight. "I don't care where he's from," Arpaio told the eager crowd in the meeting room in the Sun City West Foundation Plaza. "We are looking at a forged document. Period. I know all the politicians say, 'Sheriff, don't talk about it.' But how can I back down when we started it? I'm not going to just forget it."

Mike Zullo, the lead investigator on the case and so-called commander of Arpaio's "Cold Case Posse," told the crowd that he knew Trump's statement was a "punch in the gut, because it was unexpected." He added that he thought Trump's statement was "strategic."

"It's not going to deter us," Zullo said. "It's not going to stop us. I am closer than ever."

Zullo said that he was not sure whether Obama was born in the United States. He also said that an unnamed official high up in Kapiolani Medical Center for Women and Children in Honolulu, the hospital listed on Obama's birth certificate, had "assured me that birth never took place there, and I believe him."

The birther campaign highlighted what I knew of Donald Trump from my experience working at Trump University, in particular his penchant for creating parallel universes populated by "facts" that conformed to whatever goal he was striving for at the moment. The goal of *any business* is to make money, and his actions reflected that reality. With respect to Trump University, he really believed that this company was a "university" that somehow deserved the same status as Harvard. In Donald Trump's mind, if Donald Trump were involved in something, it was, by definition, "great." If Donald Trump accepted something as true, then it had to be true for all people. If you didn't see it his way, you were a loser or even a dangerous enemy. To validate his wild assertions, he would uncover a source and point to it, regardless of its unreliability. His sources often included blatantly ridiculous Internet rumors. For example, his remarks about the attacks of September 11 and the "cheering" crowds of Muslims in New Jersey were drawn from unfounded stories that have circulated on the web for years. The claims have been thoroughly debunked. There is no video or photographic evidence. But for months Trump stood by his story about "thousands" of Muslims celebrating, citing what his fans told him on Twitter as evidence that he was right.

At a packed campaign rally, he said, "I'm getting all of these tweets: 'I saw it.' 'I was there.' 'I was this.'" For Trump, Twitter is an instant feedback loop, giving him support for even the most defamatory assertions.

Fox News host Bill O'Reilly even advised Trump to stop tweeting after the candidate had been widely denounced for a retweet of fake crime statistics. "I retweeted somebody that was supposedly an expert," Trump told O'Reilly. When pressed by O'Reilly on the accuracy of the statement, Trump replied, "Bill, am I going to check every statistic?"

In March 2016, Trump defended his comments that a man who tried to rush the stage during a Trump rally had ties to ISIS. On NBC's "Meet the Press," he said, "Now, I don't know. What do I know about it? All I know is what's on the Internet."

That was my boss, Donald Trump. He lived in a world of his own making, and woe to anyone who told him otherwise. As for the prize money promised by Michael Sexton for getting a copy of Barack Obama's birth certificate? I never saw a penny. But I checked, I still have my personal copy.

11.

Throughout 2008 and 2009, I continued to travel to Trump University events around the country. I saw many instructors, including James Harris, Tad Lignell, Steve and Chris Goff, Denise DeVoe, David Stamper, and Billy Cannon, dispense nonsense to students. Sometimes, the students knew more than the instructors did. I even saw audience members cut off speakers or challenge them during Q&A in Boston, Orlando, and elsewhere.

I saw a woman at a workshop raise her hand. After being ignored by Harris, she interrupted him, shouting, "Stop! You can't do that!" Harris brushed her objections aside.

More than once I saw Harris, out of an excess of arrogance and embarrassment, get frustrated and angry, scolding the student and the rest of the audience on a topic that he was completely wrong about. Becoming increasingly concerned about what I was seeing, I went to Sexton and Highbloom and said, "You need a compliance auditor at these events." They wanted to know why, and I said that it was because the instructors were teaching sales unethically and that they were dispensing information that could land their students in jail.

Sexton and Highbloom didn't realize what was going on. They may have been in the dark because no one was "hand-picking" or even vetting the Trump University presenters—certainly not Donald Trump, but possibly not even Michael Sexton. Most of the instructors and mentors came to Trump University through Mark Dove, the ringmaster in the world of front-end, high-pressure speaker scams. As Corinne Sommer, manager of the Events Department (including the coordination of Trump University live events, workshops, and training) testified in her 2016 deposition, "Trump University instructors and mentors were not hand-picked by Donald Trump. I believe that in many instances Donald Trump had neither met the instructors or mentors, nor did he know who they were. Instead, I recall that Trump University hired its speakers and mentors through Mark Dove in New Hampshire, who hired and trained a number of real estate salespeople that he provided to Trump University.

These people did not necessarily have real estate experience, but they were skilled at high-pressure sales. I recall that Trump University fired two of Mike Dove's salespeople because they kept trying to get Trump University students to invest in their own personal businesses."

Although some of our lecturers and mentors had taken real estate courses, most had never even owned a home beyond their primary residence. Some were ex-convicts! It was true that mentors were giving students bad advice for personal benefit or to get them to invest in their own schemes. They would sell off their own personal real estate investments to trusting students.

I wanted Michael Sexton and April Neumann, the director of operations, to hire somebody to undertake a compliance audit of all our speakers and all of our speaking engagements. I said we needed it because we were giving bad information at these events. In certain states, students couldn't legally do what we were saying they could do.

Michael Sexton's response was disarming. He made it a challenge, saying to me, "You found the problem, so you fix it. You be the auditor!" The others agreed, saying, "Great, go do it!"

I really believed that they wanted me to fix it. I truly believed it *could* be fixed, even though this meant that we had to retrain and reeducate our mentors. We had to redo our materials and fix everything.

Until then, my home base was the Trump University headquarters at 40 Wall Street, taking phone calls. But then Sexton sent me traveling all over the United States and Canada. On weekends I was sent to workshops where the speakers knew next to nothing about real estate. My job was to take over for the speakers who were so incompetent that students were leaving because the information that was being given to them was not credible.

Maybe Sexton sent me on the road because the problems with the students and instructors were beginning to impact revenues. For Trump University, a problem that was getting in the way of making money was a problem worth fixing. The question of "quality education" was just an annoying detail.

On October 7, 2009, the Texas Consumer Protection & Public Health Division requested that Texas Attorney General Greg Abbott launch an investigation into Trump University's advertising and business practices. The letter from attorney Rick Berlin to David Morales, deputy attorney general for civil litigation, asked the attorney general to seek a settlement of $5.4 million and bar Trump University from conducting business in the state of Texas. It said, in part:

> On Thursday, September 24, 2009, Trump University placed advertisements in *The Houston Chronicle* for several "free investor workshops" to be held in the Houston area. The free workshop advertisement advises you to "Cash in on the Greatest Property Liquidation in History!" The full one-page ad claims that "2009 is the 'perfect storm' for real estate investors" and that the workshops will teach you about foreclosure investing, how to finance deals using other people's money, and quotes Donald Trump as saying, "I can turn anyone into a successful real estate investor, including you." The ad further professes that you can buy real estate from banks at up to 70% below market value. The ad, however, includes a disclaimer stating that results are not typical. The next workshop is on October 12, 2009 in Austin, Texas.

Background Facts:
Consumers on blog sites have complained that "tidbits" of information are gained at the workshops, but that the information is not worth the thousands of dollars one ultimately pays to remain in the three-day workshop after the initial "free" day. The workshop is a high stress sales pitch to pay money for the rest of the information. One consumer stated that the only things that happened at the three day workshop was:

- They pre-qualify you for a $35,000 Gold Package.
- They ask that you call your credit card company for a credit limit increase.
- They try and sell you on their mentoring services.

Trump's Deceptive Trade Practices:

- The Trump U "instructors" who appear live represent themselves as successful students of the Trump U seminar and give verbal testimonials that resemble motivational speeches about how easily they made money in real estate investing. After the video, testimonials, and motivational speech, the Trump University representatives engage in the hard sell, emphasizing to their audience that if they leave without signing up for the three-day seminar, they will not succeed using the information they learned at the "free" workshop.

- The "Gold Elite" package includes additional classes, foreclosed property search software, and a three-day meeting with one of Defendants' representatives, which are also all offered for sale independently. Consumers complain that the information is out of date, inapplicable to the Texas real estate market, and generally of little practical value. Moreover, the so-called strategies that are taught are highly speculative and may be tantamount to encouraging attendees to sell real estate without a license, which is . . . illegal in Texas.

## STEPHEN GILPIN

Donald J. Trump Is Named Individually

We have named Donald J. Trump individually because he has extensive direct involvement in this business. He is featured prominently and directly in the advertising (identified as Chairman of Trump U) and he speaks directly to the audience at the seminars, encouraging them to sign up for the courses so that they can learn his secrets to success. The ads contain an enlarged photograph of Donald Trump, who is also quoted in the ad: "'I can turn anyone into a successful real estate investor, including you.' —Donald J. Trump." The ads also promise to teach attendees "Donald Trump's powerful techniques and strategies."

Trump also signs direct mail letters to prospective attendees residing in Texas. These letters are a personal invitation from Mr. Trump to attend his class and ask the question if traders and bankers get bailouts and rescue packages, "Who's helping you? I will," states Donald Trump.

The Better Business Bureau gave the school a D-minus for 2010, its second-lowest grade, after tracking at least seventy allegations of deceptive practices from New York to Hawaii. Those included seven students saying they were pressured to max out their credit cards.

In Florida, Attorney General Bill McCollum's office began reviewing complaints from people who had paid up to $35,000 for the Trump Elite packages which promised "priceless information" that they said never came.

Trump University had begun producing large "expos" that weren't generating profits. In three weekly statements on profits and losses from 2010 Trump University seminars, Trump University showed a loss in two of them. Trump University controller Steven Matejek said in a deposition that in late 2009, Trump University was delinquent on its rent to the Trump Organization. Trump said in a deposition that he paid former students millions of dollars in refunds.

I made an appearance as a speaker at a three-day Trump University workshop at the Florida Hotel and Conference Center, near Orlando International Airport. Before arriving at the hotel, I had taken care of a small but important piece of business. It was a rule of Trump University that all speakers at live events were required to wear a wedding band. This was meant to convey a subtle message of success and stability, as well as to discourage single women from entertaining any romantic ideas about the glamorous, wealthy speaker. This was in keeping with the notion that the live events had but one purpose: to drain cash from the attendees. No distractions were tolerated. The event organizers even had a supply of plain gold rings that a ringless speaker could borrow for the weekend. But I wanted something with more bling, so on my own dime I went to Cartier and bought a gold wedding ring with inset diamonds and sapphires. For my "mug shot" to be used in the program, I had my photo taken as I was driving out of the driveway at Vanderbilt Mansion.

The hotel was hosting several unrelated events on the same day. When I walked into one of the ballrooms I saw a guy on stage trying to hypnotize the audience. I thought, "Now there's a novel approach to real estate education." After a moment I realized I was in the wrong room. The guy onstage was trying to help the audience lose weight and quit their addictions. I laughed to myself and got out of there.

I soon found the Trump University ballroom. I quickly got the feeling that I was not welcome.

The speaker, whose first name was Eric (I think he's since changed his name because of the Trump University publicity), was incensed that I was there. Feeling threatened, he knew that I had come to audit his event and that I was going to be the eyes and ears that reported what he was doing wrong back to Michael Sexton. He shouted at the event manager, "What's he doing here? He's not working my event. I don't want to be working with Steve Gilpin!"

I think that Eric was conflicted about the Trump University program. When I met him, I was struck by the fact that instead of a business suit and tie, which was the Trump uniform, he was wearing a Polo shirt with blue and white stripes, with no jacket. On page 15 of the *Trump University Sales Play Book* there appeared these instructions:

"All Trump U Team Members must be professionally dressed at least one hour prior to the beginning of the preview. Attire must always be neat, ironed and professional. All Trump U Team Members will always be dressed in a suit and must (with the exception of the Speaker) wear their jacket throughout the duration of the preview. Trump U Team Members should never have visible tattoos or facial piercings at any Trump U events." I guess Eric thought that he could "go rogue" and still be an effective salesman for Trump.

The attendees began to file in and take their seats. As I watched them, I imagined that they were expecting *magic*. They were expecting life-changing information delivered by real estate experts hand-picked by Donald Trump. They were hoping that if the stars were in alignment, Mr. Trump himself might pop in to say a few words. After all, their Preview presenter had hinted that this might happen. This is what the *Play Book* said about the three-day workshops:

> During this 3-Day Profit from Real Estate Investing workshop, students will learn strategies they need to know in order to build their fortune through real estate investing. Students will even have the opportunity to bring potential leads to class, and the instructor will do a live call on a potential deal. Students will have the opportunity to meet with a Trump U Team Member and have a one-on-one consultation, where their goals will be reviewed, and they'll discover their path to success.
>
> This 3-day Profit from Real Estate Investing workshop will teach how to:
>
> - Understand the foreclosure process
> - Locate great deals
> - Find properties
> - Create great credit
> - Structure the deal
> - Understand short sales
> - Invest in bank REOs
> - Use commercial financing
> - Build a buyer's list
> - Turn over your real estate quickly
> - And more!

Even though I wasn't supposed to go on until the next day, Eric called me up to the stage as soon as the program began. Perhaps he thought he could give me the bum's rush once I was done speaking to the students. But I insisted that he go on as scheduled and that I would wait my turn. As he dutifully took the stage, I sat in the back of the room and made mental notes of everything he was saying that was incorrect. "You can't do that!" I thought to myself. "That's wrong!"

The next day it was my turn to address the crowd. Unlike the other Trump mentors, I was a genuine real estate expert, so I wasn't worried about being able to provide information to the class. What made it difficult was that I looked out into the audience from back-stage and I recognized many of the faces. I had built my real estate business in Florida, so my former colleagues and people in the industry had come to see me. They came to see who I had become now that I was working for Donald Trump. My aunt was in the audi-ence. My ex-girlfriend was in the audience. It seemed like everyone I knew was in the audience. They wanted to know what Steve Gilpin had to say. It made me so nervous that I got leg cramps right before I had to go on. I got so nervous that I couldn't speak.

I told one of the other speakers, Omar Peru, that I didn't want to go on. Omar wasn't a Trump University mentor. He was someone who had been brought in to speak for the day. He was as qualified as I was and I respected him. He was one of the very few completely legit speakers besides me that Trump University had ever invited to an event. He knew just what to do to help calm my nerves.

"I can help you," he said. "Let's turn up the air conditioner all the way, so that you're freezing your ass off, and everybody in the audience is cold. That will wake them up. Also, let's bring the lights all the way up. Then we'll give you a long introduction. Get out there on stage and I'll take as much time as I need introducing you until you feel calm and safe."

As soon as I walked on the stage, I started choking. Everyone was looking at me—especially the people I knew. While Eric was introducing me, Omar slapped me on the back and whispered in my ear. "You're okay!" he said. "Loosen your tie."

"I've got a cramp in my foot," I whispered, forlornly.

"So take off your shoes, then," he said. "Go ahead, take off your shoes! Pull up a chair and sit backwards in the chair. Take off your jacket and throw it on the floor. Get relaxed. Then just start talking to them about real estate."

It worked. I found myself able to speak. I get so passionate about real estate that by the end of the day, you couldn't get me off the stage. Omar had saved me with his confidence, voice, and kindness. I had been set up for failure by the awful speaker of the previous day, but then, all of a sudden, I turned it around.

They kept me there for the third day but didn't put me on stage again. That's when I saw the showmanship of the thing. Naively I thought, *we're doing this to teach people about real estate*, but it was really about the money: how to sell, lower the lights, break for lunch. Everything was a sales pitch.

At the end of the Orlando weekend, I felt that I had a big job ahead of me. It was like pushing a giant boulder up a mountain. Pushing the boulder—that is, teaching the class—would be challenging enough on level ground, but the task was magnified by the fact that I was pushing against the mountain of misinformation that the other speakers were dispensing.

12.

Having taken the plunge into speaking at the workshops and discovering that I was pretty good at it, for the duration of 2009 and most of 2010 I did nothing but work in New York on weekdays and travel every weekend to a new city, doing a roadshow and talking to the audience. Even today, I get excited when I talk about real estate, and my passion is infectious. Trump University was happy with the system, because after I was done speaking, the salespeople could swoop in, do their hard sell, and close the deal on more workshops and packages. Audiences loved me and I loved the acceptance they gave me.

While on the subject of audiences, I want to take a moment to correct what I think is a false impression that has been generated by many well-meaning members of the media and critics of Trump University. There is the idea that all of our students were ignorant hayseeds, blinded by the golden aura of the god-like Trump, living in trailer parks, chewing tobacco, eating beans from a can, and looking for a miracle ticket to wealth. In my experience, this was not the case.

Most of the Trump University workshop students I met were intelligent, hard-working people who sincerely saw the program as a way of improving themselves. They were people with college degrees, retirees from big corporations, and people who were unhappy with their jobs and who were seeking a positive change. Many of them had some experience in buying and selling real estate—more experience, in many cases, than our speakers. Those who bought the Elite packages had read the descriptions carefully and were confident that the money they paid was a fair price. Indeed, in my opinion, if Trump University had properly and fully delivered what it promised in each of the Elite packages, the students actually would have received fair value for their money. The problem with Trump University wasn't that the *promises* were impossible: the problem was that the *delivery* was lacking and dangerously inaccurate.

In some cities the student investors were more knowledgeable than the average customers, so they were quicker to realize the seminar was not what they expected, and so many of them pulled out after the first day and demanded refunds. It seemed the one thing Michael Sexton was against was giving out refunds. Talking to him about refunds was like waving a silver crucifix in front of Dracula. The reaction was swift and certain. Instead, I was flown in on an emergency basis to placate and reassure angry students, and, as a side benefit, to actually teach them some genuine real estate techniques and best practices.

The huge rooms had hundreds of seminar students, which represented well over a million dollars in revenues for Trump University. They did not want to lose a penny of it. Fortunately, the students were suitably impressed by me—the expert specially flown in from Donald Trump's office to talk about real estate. They were grateful and relieved that someone with real credibility was talking to them. But as usual, the Trump University sales pitch promised more than what the organization ever intended to deliver. As I waited in the wings, the salesperson on the stage would say, "Mr. Trump's personal advisor is coming in to see you, ladies and gentlemen! This is the man who sits next to the man!" They set expectations so high that no one could have lived up to it.

I was never Donald Trump's personal advisor. In fact, at that time I had only ever met Donald Trump once. It was quite by accident. I was waiting for the elevator in the Trump Building at 40 Wall Street. I was alone. Suddenly, just as the elevator door pinged open, a group of executives swept around the corner and headed in my direction. High above the other heads—Trump is six-foot two—I saw the distinctive orange hair. I entered the elevator and they followed. The doors closed. Trump was standing next to me. He caught my eye. I extended my hand. "Hello, Mr. Trump," I said. "Steve Gilpin."

He nodded but did not shake my hand. I was not surprised. Donald Trump doesn't like to touch people. A self-confessed germaphobe, Trump doesn't even like to push an elevator button because of lurking bacteria. Trump especially avoids shaking hands with teachers, since they are likely to be have been in contact with lots of unwashed, germy kids.

In his 1997 book *The Art of the Comeback*, Trump wrote, "One of the curses of American society is the simple act of shaking hands, and the more successful and famous one becomes the worse this terrible custom seems to get. I happen to be a clean hands freak. I feel much better after I thoroughly wash my hands, which I do as much as possible."

Trump has what he calls a borderline case of germaphobia—also known as mysophobia—that the American Psychological Association defines as one of the more common forms of obsessive-compulsive disorder. Symptoms include fanatical self-cleaning, usually hand scrubbing, after every contact with potential germs. In the elevator, Donald Trump looked at me and said, "Hello, Mr. Gilpin." He would later testify under oath in a deposition that he did not know me. I guess I'm just a forgettable kind of guy.

Having been falsely introduced to the workshop audience as a man who had a relationship with Donald Trump, I would do my best to teach the audience specific types of real estate transactions, and to give solid evidence tied to the data for what works and what doesn't. I liked to use numbers to back up my suggestions and calculations.

At a workshop at the Hilton Hotel in Melville, New York—a town thirty miles east of Manhattan on the Long Island Expressway—the speaker there was a man named Billy Cannon. As I watched his presentation, I quickly saw that he was giving incorrect information. Students complained about him. I felt I had to take over the event, because I didn't want to go to jail with Billy. I, too, was representing Trump University and teaching its program.

Michael Sexton tried to rescue the workshop by getting someone from *Celebrity Apprentice* to come over. Because Sexton didn't know anyone at *Celebrity Apprentice*, it's my assumption that Donald Trump therefore was involved. It's likely he knew that the speaker for this lecture was going off the rails. I asked Billy to leave.

His response was curious. He said, "Steve, there's nothing you can do. You can't save this group. There's no money to be made here. Let's end the event and hit the bar. We can watch the game on television."

"We can't just walk away," I replied. "We owe them an education! People paid for this workshop and the course. It's education, not just selling. You have to *teach* them something. They paid fifteen hundred bucks and you want to leave and watch a football game because you think there's no more money to be made? So what if there's no money to be made? Just do the education!" Billy left the room and went to a bar to watch the football game.

I was able to calm the audience down by teaching them something real. I started with a moment of truth. I went back to the audience, looked out at the students, and said to them, "This is very simple. There should be a mathematical return on your real estate investment that makes sense financially. Let's go through the numbers that Billy has been providing you with today." So we went through Billy's numbers.

Then I said, "Now let's do the numbers my way, and you'll realize the correct ROI." I wanted them to understand that if someone presents a deal to you, you'd better do the math.

The deal Billy had been offering didn't work, but he had made it sound delicious. He had even browbeat the audience, saying, "Why wouldn't you want to invest in this? Are you *stupid*?" That's the type of demeanor this man had. His attitude was that if you didn't like it or you didn't want to do it his way, then he didn't want to help you. The audience was shocked, of course, that I had challenged Billy's logic, but by throwing him under the bus and telling the truth as I saw it, I re-established trust and kept many students from leaving.

Then I had an idea. I called April Neumann and said, "If you want to save this, we need to do a bus tour and call it a profit lab." She agreed. It was the first bus tour I did at Trump University.

The bus tour worked and I saved the event. We sold packages to more than twenty-five percent of the audience, and we did it legally, ethically, and by actually educating the students. This experience, more than anything else, convinced me that Trump University could be saved. We just had to enact new policies and hire new mentors. We needed to teach only in the states that allowed creative financing and quick turnarounds, and we needed to avoid the states where it was discouraged or illegal. Trump University just needed to restructure how they did things and what states they did them in. This would have saved them from lawsuits. They should have apologized for what they'd taught so far, taken responsibility, offered refunds to former students, and then moved on, providing honest educations. It would have prevented further scandals.

But I also saw the signs of decay. My role in saving the seminar was not acknowledged. Billy got his cut, and I was seen as a pest, the guy who had taught too much to the students, who was giving away secrets and getting in the way of package sales.

My commission was supposed to be five percent of the gross sales, or $8,507.38, but Billy took my sales and I got screwed out of my paycheck and bonus. Let's do the math: $8,500 is five percent of $170,000, which is what we sold that day while Billy went to the bar and drank and watched a football game. That horrible experience made me realize that something was seriously wrong with the management at Trump University. How many times was I going to need to save the school and save the students? In fact, my expertise only created a way for them to upsell students and make them think there really was something worth learning there. I was arbitrating which transactions that were being taught were legal and which were not legal, and this made me a premium mentor. As the *Trump University Sales Play Book* says on page 126: "Give them credit for taking a great first step, but don't let them think three days will be enough to make them successful. Use doctors or lawyers as an example, or any profession that requires time, money, and the right education for success. If all Trump U team members are following these procedures it will greatly improve our chances to sell Elite packages. Even one coordinator giving them the impression three days is enough that can hurt sales. People will always take the path of least resistance; do not give them the option."

When I was at an event, I was proof that this stuff was not easy to learn. I was an example for what they might become. The selling was relentless, and it was made easier by the registration forms the prospects had been asked to fill out and by the steady probing by the friendly Trump University sales staff.

Students who bought a coaching package would be able to choose which mentor would counsel them. We had twenty-eight mentors available, but students would ask for me because they had seen me on stage. "I want to work with Steve," they would say. "Steve Gilpin, the one who works with Trump."

I ended up being chosen by 5,509 students. It was an impossible number of students for me to handle over just a few years, but it was only a fraction of the students who passed through Trump University. I could not save them all.

13.

One day, I got an unexpected call from Michael Sexton.

"Do you know Canadian law?" he said.

He told me he'd sent a speaker from the United States to Canada, but the guy didn't know Canadian law and legal terms. If you're speaking to a Canadian audience you have to make sure that you use the correct Canadian terminology, because it affects the meaning and nuances of the law. Students in the Canadian class knew immediately that their speaker wasn't qualified, because he wasn't using the right jargon. For example, what you'd call a "lease option" in the United States is called a "lease back" or a "lease take back" in Canada. Before lunch on the first day of this multi-day seminar, students were already walking out of the event. It was about to be a disaster and a huge missed opportunity for sales.

So Michael Sexton sent me to the rescue. I had less than twenty-four hours to get a passport, write a guide to creative financing in the Canadian real estate market, and take over for the next two days in front of five hundred Canadian students.

Afterwards, students corralled me in a nearby restaurant, because they were so eager to meet a true real estate expert. I was stuck there until the wee hours because they were buying me drinks and would not let me go home.

There was another emergency in Philadelphia. The speaker was incompetent. He was talking about clouding deeds, doing lease options, and doing wholesale transactions. In other states, such as Rhode Island, the laws are very lax. You could sign the contract as long as you got a closing, or you could do a double escrow double close, as long as you disclosed it. But not in Pennsylvania.

I stepped in and took over. But then came another surprise. After two hours, April Neumann, Trump U. director of operations, came to the stage and demanded that I step down. I asked her what the problem was, and she said, "Because they *like* you. You're giving it all away for *free*. Stop teaching them. We need to upsell packages, to make money. We're here to *sell*."

I was shocked. April Neumann didn't want me to properly teach these students? It seemed she preferred the unqualified lecturer who had never owned a home? I was an expert with decades of experience who had bought and sold hundreds of homes. In Pennsylvania, I said, we needed to follow the Board of Realtors. The law stated that all buyers and sellers must be disclosed. But I had no choice: Neumann outranked me. I stepped down.

By this point, I had reported to Sexton and Neumann numerous cases of speakers teaching strategies that were illegal in certain states, and was confused that speakers were continuing to teach wrong information after I had complained about it. Were they not updating the speakers? I had to finally admit that it truly was all about sales. They didn't want to hinder the salespeople from upselling more courses and packages to their students. The wholesaling and other quick turnaround techniques they were teaching were core to the workshops. Without these techniques, they wouldn't attract as many students, and they wouldn't inspire them to buy more courses. It took me some time to realize that the problems were systemic, not just the actions of a few bad apples.

During my last two years at Trump University, I was not only the inside adviser, coach and mentor, I was working seven days a week. I was doing sessions and the hotline Monday through Thursday from twelve noon to eight in the evening. On Thursday night at eight o'clock, I was doing the webcast and got paid extra for it. Then, on the weekends, I would fly to a different city to support the live workshops.

I didn't mind doing the road shows until I realized, *I'm getting used here! They're just using me to pacify angry students and limit the number of refunds and lawsuits.* I was still responsible for handling calls that came in on the hotline, as well. The steady stream of complaints on the Trump University hotline became a flood.

I realized that the mentors who were hired to do these three-day events were unethical. It seemed to me they were tricking people who had paid good money to learn about real estate. These mentors were promoting real estate practices that were often unhelpful at best to hundreds of thousands of students. There was no way that I could plug all the holes in this dike.

People were starting to post complaints online. Here's one dated December 25, 2008 that was posted on the website Ripoff Report. It represents the personal opinion of the student, a man named Thomas from California. When I read this complaint, the words rang true:

I attended a real estate seminar in CA in 2008. The speaker was Denise DeVoe, supposedly a guru who has been investing for 30+ years. While this may be true, she certainly did not have a grasp on the current market condition and, after intense digging, is not a very savvy investor after all.

I learned that she has multiple lis pendens [pending legal actions] and foreclosures and that she's completely and utterly broke. This is the person who supposedly is there to teach us how to get rich. Yeah right, she's doing it for the hefty commission paid by ignorant students who listen to her sales pitch. I can't believe no one researches her before buying her product—it's all public record. Just listen to her talk, go to the public record databases in the areas she talks about, and search for her name.

At face value, the mentor program seems great. When I contacted the company for testimonials, none of them showed that a client got a single property! After speaking with people in the class about the program, they were unanimously disappointed with the level of communication, service, and results. We're paying $20,000 to be disappointed!

You would think that someone getting paid thousands of dollars for a three-day event would be more focused on delivering information, not sappy stories about dead mothers and poor people winning the lottery. She shouldn't complain about things that happened to her or how her weight is out of control. How about some professionalism??!

The whole company operates like it's out of a garage. Ms. Devoe didn't know the next event date, and the company didn't even know where my event was being held. My materials didn't arrive until three weeks after the event, after several phone calls and emails and threats. A few days after the event, I got pitched a watered down version of the mentor and a handful of other equally overpriced products for discounted rates.

Don't get me started on the Nevada lawyer she recommends. They charge $10,000 for what you can get for $2,000 in your own state or through a reputable Nevada firm. And no, you don't get what you pay for. She spent so much time defending this company on her blog, she must be getting a hefty commission from them too.

I'm not interested in a lawsuit, just keeping others from wasting money.

Thomas Undisclosed,
California U.S.A.

Of course, Trump University offered a very different assessment of Ms. Devoe. In a full-page ad in the *Washington Post Express* on July 2007, Denise Devoe was introduced like this:

Your Trump University Instructor:
Denise DeVoe

Ms. Devoe has built a vast empire of investment real estate spanning the United States, including residential, commercial, and resort properties. An innovator in foreclosure investing, she has consulted with several national banks and lending institutions such as Wells Fargo, Bank of America, and Wachovia.

"Vast empire of investment real estate" or "completely and utterly broke"? That's quite a difference of opinion—and characteristic of the wildly divergent perceptions of Trump University.

I also heard many horror stories of Trump University speakers and mentors steering students towards dubious investments in which they had a direct relationship—a blatant conflict of interest. Here's one from 2007, which was reported in May 2016 by Paul Van Osdol at WTAE-TV in Pittsburgh.

A woman named Melissa Norris of Franklin Park, PA., spent $17,248 for a Trump University seminar in Florida. The seminar was run by Prosper Learning, a company licensed by Trump University. The Provo, Utah-based company billed itself as "one of the most trusted names in one-to-one personalized education." It's often referred to as a coaching floor or a call center, but the term that many people use is "boiler room."

Norris's tuition covered a coach assigned to help her find real estate deals. Cary Beagley, of Utah, was her coach. He's well known to Utah law enforcement: in July 2011 he was charged with multiple felonies for theft and securities fraud. The complaint read, "In July 2007, Beagley, who was working for the Trump University and/or a company called Prosper Learning, Inc. as a real estate coach, began to raise money from at least three of his real estate students for various investment opportunities. Further Beagley is a person who at all pertinent times resided in Salt Lake County, Utah. In return for $150,000 from the three individuals, Beagley offered various profits in return for the funds." Norris wanted to invest in Pittsburgh real estate, but she said Beagley tried to get her to buy properties in Spain. "And that's when I became very concerned," Norris said.

But like thousands of other students, she trusted Trump University, because Donald Trump had said repeatedly, "These are all people that are hand-picked by me." Beagley told Norris to put her money into a company called Safevest, and she did. Eventually, she invested $230,000.

But just six months later, the SEC called Safevest a fraud and a Ponzi scheme and won a court order shutting it down. Beginning in May 2007, Safevest had raised $25.7 million from 550 people—specifically, Christians—to invest in non-existent commodity futures pools. The lure was profits of 1.5 percent to 1.9 percent per day, which would equal several hundred percent per year. In its prospectus, Safevest claimed that it never had a losing day. But Safevest had a big losing day eventually—it ended up bankrupt, and Norris lost all her money.

"I lost a lot of money because I trusted this organization and I have nothing back. I will not get anything back," she said. Of course, when asked about Beagley's connections to Trump, Trump's attorney Jill Martin said that Trump and Trump University "did not ever hire Beagley or engage him as a contractor." If he were being paid by Prosper Learning, then technically this may have been true.

Reporters discovered that Beagley had a criminal record including convictions for theft, drug distribution, and sex solicitation. In fact, he was still on federal probation for the drug case while he was working for Trump University. Also, he had filed Chapter 7 bankruptcy. Norris knew none of that until a reporter from WTAE-TV told her. "I want to throw up right now," she replied.

There were many mentors like Beagley who misused their positions to influence investments by students, and many students who, once they discovered the truth, felt just like Melissa Norris.

I received this from Donald Trump's secretary on behalf of Donald Trump for doing a great job on a three-day in-field mentorship with two students in New Haven, CT. Photo courtesy Stephen Gilpin.

I received this MVP award at a company awards party on January 11, 2009, for outstanding work. Photo courtesy Stephen Gilpin.

A slide from the presentation used for Profit Lab classes at paid preview events. Photo courtesy Stephen Gilpin.

Me at an Orlando, Florida "Profit from Real Estate" Trump event in June 2010, at which I was one of the two main speakers. Photo courtesy Stephen Gilpin.

Michael Cohen

From: Stephen Gilpin
Sent: Monday, August 15, 2011 9:14 PM
To: Michael Cohen
Subject: FW: Trump Entrepreneur Initiative - Mentor Steve Gilpin

Dear Atty Michael Cohen,

I was asked to forward this to you, on behalf of one of our students.

Please refer to below.

All the best

Stephen J. Gilpin
Trump Initiative
40 Wall Street
New York, Ny 10005

Cell :

STEPHEN — GREAT JOB! THANKS [signed] Donald Trump

From:
Sent: Monday, August 15, 2011 9:06 PM
To: Donald J. Trump
Cc: Mark Covais; Stephen Gilpin;
Subject: Trump Entrepreneur Initiative - Mentor Steve Gilpin

Dear Mr. Trump,

I wanted to take the time to write you regarding the valuable employee you have in Steve Gilpin. My business partner and I just completed our 3 day mentorship with Steve in New Haven, CT and it was outstanding. Steve's passion for investing in the real estate market was infectious. We had such a great time with him and shared in the excitement. The time we spent with Steve and the knowledge we gained was immeasurable. He allayed our fears about starting our business in the real estate industry. As a result of our mentorship, we made offers and one has been accepted at the time of this writing.

We would not be where we are without Steve's advice and counsel. What a stellar employee you have within your company. Steve rocks!

By copy to Steve, our sincere thank you for what you have done for us.

Sincerely,

After a three-day in-field mentorship in New Haven, one of my students sent this letter to Donald Trump (August, 2011). Photo courtesy Stephen Gilpin.

Successful Entrepreneurs...

- Must Focus on ROI not $ Signs
- Must Invest in Ongoing Training
- Must Invest in Themselves
- Must be Willing to Get in the Game
- Must Trust Someone........

A slide from the presentation used for Profit Lab classes at paid preview events. Photo courtesy Stephen Gilpin.

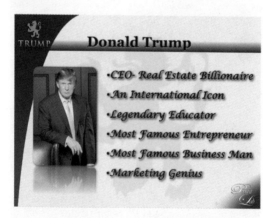

Donald Trump

- CEO- Real Estate Billionaire
- An International Icon
- Legendary Educator
- Most Famous Entrepreneur
- Most Famous Business Man
- Marketing Genius

A slide from the presentation used for Profit Lab classes at paid preview events. Photo courtesy Stephen Gilpin.

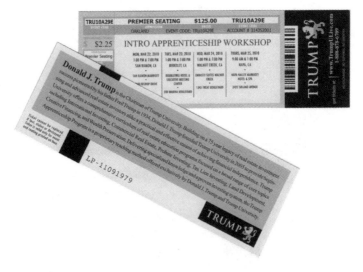

Along with invitational letters, tickets were mailed to potential clients around the country announcing a "special event" in their area. Photo courtesy Stephen Gilpin.

14.

Trump University, like many other schools, asked its students to fill out student surveys. These were supposed to be a method to get feedback from the students on the quality of their education. The surveys were handed out to workshop participants, collected, and then forwarded to the head office at 40 Wall Street.

The complex process for handling the surveys would have made Dilbert proud. According to the 2007 *Trump University Sales Play Book*, Liliana Hernandez in the accounting department passed the surveys onto Denise Ong, the live events coordinator, for survey analysis. Denise Ong compiled the survey analysis before emailing the completed survey analysis to the event report distribution list and the team which had been reviewed in the surveys. Brad Schneider—my original boss, with customer service—received the survey analysis stapled and clipped at the top of the pile. He reviewed and addressed any pertinent issues with the customer support team and client advisors before passing the surveys onto the big kahuna: April Neumann, the director of operations. She reviewed and addressed any pertinent issues with the program coordinator, sales coordinators, and speakers. Any scores of less than ninety percent would be deemed below standards and addressed through a mandated post-conference call with the team to review compliance and event expectations.

Nearly every student who attended a workshop completed a survey. The Trump Organization has ten thousand of them in their files.

In August 2008, a young woman named Tarla Makaeff attended Trump University's three- day Fast Track to Foreclosure Workshop. It cost her $1,495, which Makaeff later said she had split with a friend. Makaeff later described the Los Angeles workshop as a slick production featuring carefully choreographed presentations, speakers blaring "For the Love of Money"—the theme song from Trump's hit reality television series *The Apprentice*—and Trump University representatives exhorting students to raise their credit card limits, ostensibly to facilitate real estate transactions, but actually to enable the purchase of the $34,995 Trump Gold Elite Program.

Page 104 of the *Trump University Sales Play Book* says: "If you do discuss an attendee's accomplishments, use the conversation to your advantage. Ask how much positive cash flow they have coming in each month and how much they would like to have coming in each month. Ask if their properties are all protected in an LLC or some sort of entity. Ask if they currently have the liquid (cash) available to accomplish their goals, or to do they need an extra ten to twenty deals in the next twelve months? Ask how many real estate deals they have sold over the last six months. Ask about the vacancy or occupancy rate. Ask if that property is working for them or if they are working for that property. With what they have this minute, are they in a position to live the life they want and never have to work another day again in their life?"

Makaeff was persuaded, and she paid $34,995 to enroll in the Gold Elite Program. This entitled her to four three-day Advanced Training Workshops, a three-day Mentoring Session in the Field, and training publications, software, and other materials.

On September 28, she filled out a Field Mentor Evaluation Form. Her review was glowing. Her mentors were Rick McNally and Mike Kasper. On a scale of one (unsatisfactory) to five (excellent), she gave straight "fives" to every question about her field training: finding neighborhoods, finding deals, writing contracts, and more. Her written comments were effusive, and she described the overall experience as "amazing."

When asked to describe her best experience during the training, Makaeff wrote, "Just working with Rick and Mike in general. Both very knowledgeable, personable and outgoing. I'm very inspired by them and am looking forward to staying in touch with them. They are the best mentors ever!!!"

On October 24, 2008, Makaeff attended a workshop at the Sheraton Park Hotel at the Anaheim Resort in Anaheim, California. Again she awarded the school "fives" in every category—quality of the presentation, relevance of the topics covered, usefulness of the information, quality of the instructor. When asked, "What did you like most about the seminar?" she wrote, "Hybrid trusts—didn't know they existed. Loved hearing from CPA and attorney."

On November 2, she completed a third survey after attending a three-day Creative Financing Real Estate Workshop in Los Angeles,

California. The speaker was Tim Gorsline and the team leader was Christy Duckett. Like her other surveys, it was glowing. She handed out scores of "five," and indicated that she would attend another Trump University seminar and recommend Trump University to a friend.

On May 10, 2009 a student named Art Cohen submitted his survey after attending the Fast Track to Foreclosure Training workshop in Van Nuys, California. The speaker was James Harris. The staff team consisted of Cory Lignell (the son of Tad Lignell), Ryan Lotman, and Tiffany Brinkman. He gave the program "fours" and "fives," noting of James Harris's performance, "I already had very high expectations! He did a great job!"

On September 27, 2009, Bob Guillo provided an equally positive survey after attending the Profit from Real Estate Investing workshop in New York. The speaker was James Harris. The team members were Ryan Lotman, Cory Lignell, Scott Leitzell, Michael Hinson, Zac Hernandez, and Tiffany Brinkman. He gave the event straight "fives." He did note, however, that the room could have benefited from "more comfortable chairs."

The Trump Organization created a website called "98percentapproval.com" in 2016 to showcase the ten thousand positive surveys submitted by students. The website is no longer operating.

How could anyone explain the jarring disconnect between the effusive student surveys and the endless stream of misery and anger that flowed out of the hotline every day and which I was expected to make right? Why were these same supposedly happy students calling me with their tales of woe? There were many reasons.

As noted on page 40 of the *Play Book*, event staff were required to "distribute surveys to all attendees and collect once completed in exchange for certificates." That's right. Each student was handed a survey to fill out, and he or she did not receive their course completion certificate *until the survey had been completed and turned in.* The exchange was clear: you fill out the form and then we'll give you your certificate. Students have stated that the Trump team members would hover over them while they filled out the forms, making it more awkward for them to write anything critical.

The Trump survey forms have lines for the student's name, email address, and phone number. On some of the forms these are noted as "optional," but on many of the forms this is not stated. This is how we know which surveys were filled out by Makaeff, Cohen, Guillo, and the others—because their names are written at the tops of the pages, and often their signatures appear at the bottoms.

In every normal college, teacher evaluation forms are *strictly confidential.* The student fills out the form and the only identifier is the name of the teacher and the class. This encourages candor, because it's difficult for the teacher to figure out which student, if any, made a negative comment.

Students have also said that Trump team members went so far as to plead with students to submit positive reviews, saying that if they got negative reviews, they'd be fired or have their pay cut. Trump University mentor Tad Lignell told the *New York Times* that he asked students to fill out the evaluations in front of him at restaurants or coffee shops. At that moment, vulnerable students still needed and expected his guidance. As they filled out the forms, their mindset was, "I want my mentor to be my friend and I need his help." Virtually all his students, he said, gave him the top rating of "five." But had they not, his income ($5,500 per student signed up, and later $4,500) could have been in jeopardy. He said that Trump University managers made clear that teachers with low ratings would be passed over in favor of those with high scores. "That puts an emphasis on getting fives," he said. "If you wanted more students, you knew you needed those."

Incidentally, Lignell also told the newspaper that Trump University had failed to pay him for several students. "If Trump wins the presidency," he said, "I've got a president who owes me fifty thousand dollars." It seems as though the Trump practice of stiffing people who work for him extended to his own "hand-picked" mentors.

The second reason why there were so many positive reviews is that hostages have positive feelings toward their captors, sometimes to the point of defending and identifying with the captors. These feelings are generally considered irrational in light of the danger or risk endured by the victims. In other words, immersed in the glitz and glamour of the fancy ballroom event, with carefully trained high-pressure salespeople hovering at their elbow, many students were swept up with positive feelings that, in the cold light of day, turned sour.

On April 17, Judge Kim McLane Wardlaw of the United States Court of Appeals for the Ninth Circuit in Pasadena, California, in ruling that Trump University could not sue Tarla Makaeff for defamation, wrote this:

> On appeal, Trump University nevertheless argues that
> Makaeff's early testimonials praising Trump University

indirectly prove that she acted with a high degree of awareness of the probable falsity of her later statements. (While still in the program, Makaeff described Trump University's programs as "amazing" and "excellent" on rating sheets provided by Trump University. Later, in June 2009, she was videotaped at a workshop praising her mentor and saying favorable things about Trump University.)

However, it is plausible that Makaeff sincerely believed in Trump University's offerings when she submitted her written and videotaped testimonials. The gist of Makaeff's complaint about Trump University is that it constitutes an elaborate scam. As the recent Ponzi-scheme scandals involving one-time financial luminaries like Bernard Madoff and Allen Stanford demonstrate, victims of con artists often sing the praises of their victimizers until the moment they realize they have been fleeced.

Makaeff's initial enthusiasm for Trump University's program is not probative of whether she acted with actual malice.

The key phrase is, "victims of con artists often sing the praises of their victimizers until the moment they realize they have been fleeced." So true!

Remember that much of the value of Trump University Elite packages was based on the promise of *future delivery* of services by the school. The Gold Elite three-day personal mentorship, the access to Foreclosure DealSource and the Wealth Builder's Network (WBN) (both White Labeled), the promised seminars—all of these were benefits that you'd receive long after you forked over your $34,995. It's no surprise, therefore, that a student's initial enthusiasm, expressed while the super-friendly Trump team member was leaning over their shoulder, would, as the weeks and months passed, turn into bitter disappointment and the feeling of having been cheated.

It also appears that Trump University team members directly meddled in the review process. More than one student has reported that they were pressured to upgrade their reviews after they had turned them in. John Brown, a plaintiff in the Makaeff lawsuit, is a resident of New York City and has a BA in psychology and an MS in education. At the time of his deposition, he was sixty-one years old. He paid for the Trump University courses in the hopes that he could build a retirement fund that would protect him in the later years of his life. He truly believed the Trump sales pitch: for a significant investment, he would gain access to the proprietary inside knowledge that helped Donald Trump stay on top of the real estate game. In his mind, it was not unlike paying to attend reputable classes in law or engineering.

Brown was not satisfied with his mentorship. After the mentorship, his mentor asked him to evaluate the mentorship with scores of one to five. Brown awarded the mentorship mostly average scores of "three," because he believed the information they provided was basic and mediocre.

The next day a Trump University representative called Brown, asking him to change his average scores to "fives." Brown believes it was either Diego Guevera or Jason Schauer who contacted him. Brown refused. The person called back two more times. Tired of the continuing phone calls, Brown finally gave in and agreed that Trump University could change his ratings to "fives." In a letter to

Trump University dated June 11, 2011, Brown complained of this and demanded a refund. Needless to say, he didn't get one.

There have even been allegations that survey forms were forged. In March 2016, the *Palm Beach Post* published a story about Charles Jacobson, a Florida retiree who in 2009 heard about a Trump University workshop offered at a West Palm Beach hotel. Hoping he could dramatically improve his financial fortunes, he attended, and bought the Trump Gold Elite package for twenty-six thousand dollars, which he put on his American Express card.

Jacobson said a mentor accompanied him on trips around the area, where they looked at various property listings. The plan, as Jacobson remembered it, was to somehow buy real estate without cash, sell it quickly, and pocket the profits. "Nothing came of it," Jacobson said. "He defrauded us all."

Jill Martin, an attorney for the Trump Organization, disputed Jacobson's contention that the course was a scam, and pointed out that Jacobson had provided positive reviews. "Mr. Jacobson was not only satisfied," she emailed the paper, "but even went so far as to indicate that he wanted to share his positive experience with Trump University in its monthly magazine." Martin's email included two evaluation forms she said Jacobson completed.

Reviewing the forms, Jacobson said he remembered completing a portion of the first form, dated October 1, 2009, though he said the date was incorrect. He reported on the form that his overall experience was "excellent" and praised the work of his mentor, listed as Chris Lombardo.

Jacobson said he did not sign or date the form. The numerical ratings for various aspects of the course were all "fives." He also did not check the box asking if he'd like to "share your success story with Trump University."

The second, longer form was dated October 5, 2009. In handwriting that is markedly different from the earlier form, the course gets glowing reviews, with more praise for Lombardo. Aspects of the course are again given the highest possible ratings, and this time the writer says "yes" when asked if he would like to share his success story with Trump University. "This is not my handwriting," Jacobson told newspaper. "Not even close."

Eventually, Jacobson declared bankruptcy. The money he shelled out for the Trump University course "was the main factor," he said. "Try paying off twenty-six thousand dollars to American Express when you don't have anything coming in." Is the second review form a forgery? You can see them online and judge for yourself. There are links in the *Palm Beach Post* article from March 5, 2016, titled "$26,000 loss to Trump University makes disabled Florida man 'nauseous.'"

15.

As the months dragged on and I flew around the country putting out one fire after another, I increasingly realized that I needed to fight the management of Trump University. I felt responsible for my unhappy students, but there were now so many of them that I couldn't possibly answer all of their questions or fix all of the mistakes that the mentors were making. I thought we needed to fire most of our mentors before they got us sued. More importantly, I was outraged that our students, many of whom had become friends, and all of whom I felt protective of, seemed to have been victims of fraud. Something had to be done.

I always assumed that because Trump University CEO Michael Sexton was ignorant of the business of real estate, it was his own lack of expertise that led him to hire unqualified lecturers and mentors. I figured he just wanted to get the school up and running and make it profitable as quickly as possible, and that he stuffed the roster with motivational speakers because they could be hired and trained easily. But as student complaints mounted, and as I kept being flown from one dysfunctional workshop to another, I began to wonder: was the hiring process simply inept, or was something else going on?

I had once believed that management genuinely wanted to change Trump University structurally, but in hindsight, I now believe they were just using me to take all the money they could get before the organization inevitably folded.

There have been suggestions that Trump University was in fact a Ponzi scheme. For instance, if the Elite packages had been fulfilled as promised, the company might have lost money. The only endgame, I guess, was to *not* fulfill the packages—which was pretty much what the company was doing—and instead to use incoming money to placate students who complained and keep them from suing or creating bad publicity. No matter how you looked at it, as it was designed and was being operated, Trump University was unsustainable. This was made even more inevitable by the money that Trump was taking out of it.

I still believed that they could fix it. I insisted to Michael that Trump University had to start giving out refunds to students they had educated wrong. I emailed all the mentors with corrections, saying, "You can't do this, you can't do that." I started documenting the Trump University hotline calls using a coaching dashboard where the student who called could see the problem they reported and what we were doing to fix it.

They should have given students free coaching sessions to fix mentor errors. They should have gotten rid of the mentors that didn't know real estate. But they couldn't get rid of problem mentors like James Harris (the mentor who was also a convicted felon for aggravated assault for intentionally ramming his truck into another truck), because James Harris was a sales superstar. At seminars he would upsell twenty-five percent of the audience, bringing in millions of dollars at each event. If Michael Sexton got rid of instructors like James Harris, his business model wouldn't work. For a while, to promote himself and Trump University, James Harris wrote a blog. Here's one entry from February 17, 2010.

What Makes James Harris Trump U's Biggest Money Motivator?

James Harris will tell you that when it comes down to it, anyone can create wealth in real estate with the right education. Harris's can-do attitude is certainly convincing. Be it in one of his two-hour lectures or a three-day seminar, this guy's directness, factual know-how, and big-city flair will put you on the right track—and motivate you to stay there.

It's not just an act, either. Sure, he seems like the kind of guy you would want around all the time—be it as a golf partner or mentoring your first big investment deals. But he also has more that fifteen years of real estate industry experience. The things you learn from him in hands-on learning session and easy-to-understand teaching points are proven successful. His student's find him fun and enthralling James Harris is during his instructing sessions (sic), and this is never truer than when he is providing the tools to work through real-world situations.

Can't attend a session any time soon? Follow the James Harris Trump University Twitter @MoneyMotivatorl for daily information on real estate investments and wealth management.

Here's his post from February 24, 2010. He restates the same pitch that I heard him give when he told students what their new license plate slogan would be:

Learn How Your Catch Phrase Can Be "Paid For"

"Paid for." That's what James Harris and Trump University promise you will be chanting after your time spent working with the educational programs at Trump University. And how could you not? The lecture series that James Harris runs, ranging from a few hours of real estate tips to a few days of bare-bones entrepreneurial know-how, contains everything that you are going to need to know about growing your wealth and then managing it.

Investing in real estate is not an easy thing—nor does one seminar session guarantee millions of dollars coming your way. But arming yourself with the information James Harris provides, assimilating it, and finding the right team of smart and talented colleagues is the way that the sports car you have been dreaming of will drive off the lot with the license plate reading "PAID FOR"—and with you behind the wheel.

And here's one from April 15, 2010 telling students how to evict a tenant:

Eviction Advice from James Harris & Trump U

As one of Trump University's main instructors, James Harris has covered every aspect of real estate investing and he'll be the first to tell you there's a right way and a wrong way to evict a tenant. If you are currently renting property to a tenant, always be prepared to take back your property quickly and legally at all times. James Harris always says, "You need to protect your property. It's your greatest asset." When the time comes to terminate your rental agreement with a tenant, your first step as a property owner is to deliver proper notice. Depending on the state laws, if the tenant violates his or her obligations to pay rent, the landlord may instigate the eviction by delivering a note to the tenant at least 20 days in advance of the end of the month.

However, if the tenant is being evicted due to a rule that excludes children on the property, or if the home is to be converted to condominiums, then the landlord must deliver a notice of eviction at least 90 days in advance.

Under no circumstances is it proper or legal to change the locks or shut down the utilities to force tenants out of your property. Even if your property lease states you can change the locks or evict without notice, many states that follow the Landlord-Tenant Act will not uphold your contract.

If the tenant refuses to comply with the original eviction notice, the landlord must file a lawsuit to evict the tenant. Many states call this "An Action in Forcible Entry and Detainer." Next, a court official will serve the tenant a notice of the court date, and a judge will enter a monetary judgment to recoup the lost payments.

Take this advice from James Harris and Trump University because if you miss any of these steps in the eviction process, the tenant can file an appeal to delay the process, or make you start over from the beginning.

This advice can be found anywhere online at no cost. There is absolutely no reason to pay anyone a penny for it. My guess is that Harris, who himself possessed scant knowledge of real estate laws and procedures, simply did what anyone else would do—he Googled the subject and slapped together a quick blog post. There's nothing there that anyone with a high school education couldn't produce.

I was angry because these mentors, who didn't know real estate, were making a twenty-five percent commission on the audience, and I wasn't getting paid anything extra to tour the company and clean up after them. Trump University didn't value my ability to educate students. They were actually starting to see it as a *problem*, because by teaching them something real I was interfering with students' need to buy more courses. The management must have known that Trump University could not be fixed without losing money. Teaching the students correctly cost too much. So they decided to bring in the money now, and decided to deal with the consequences later.

I don't even blame James Harris. He may not have delivered what the students wanted—but he delivered *exactly what Trump University expected*. Michael Sexton and David Highbloom didn't want educators running the seminars. They had gotten rid of the educators in 2007, just before they had hired me to be the only qualified real estate expert in the company. All the rest of the qualified people were gone, replaced by motivational speakers and hard-sell salespeople.

"I was told to do one thing," said Harris in an interview with the *Washington Post*. "And that one thing was . . . to show up to teach, train, and motivate people to purchase the Trump University products and services and make sure everybody bought. That is it." I couldn't agree more. If you *want* a shark, you *hire* a shark, and you shouldn't be surprised when the shark does exactly what sharks do. And as for being "handpicked" by Donald Trump—which is what Harris often told his workshop students—Harris said he met Trump once in the early 1990s, backstage at an event at the Taj Mahal casino. "Here is the truth," he said. "When I was at Trump University, I had not one interaction with him ever. Not one."

When the Trump Organization heard what Harris said in his interview, a Trump spokesman said Harris's comments had "no merit" and accused Harris of "looking for media attention to further his own agenda." I thought Harris was being honest.

16.

One day, I was on a podcast taking place in the Trump University offices on the thirty-second floor of 40 Wall Street. Donald Trump was participating from another office. We were talking about the real estate market, and whether it was a fire sale right now. I was panicking a little about my job, looking at the market. Trump said, "Steve, first off look where you're at, and look who you're with. If the real estate market is a fire sale, I'm sitting right next to you, who do you think they're getting first?" Coincidentally, the building actually caught on fire that day. So we had to stop the podcast and get out of the building by climbing down thirty-two flights of stairs.

At the time, Sexton was interviewing people who wrote courses on tax deeds, tax sales, and tax liens. He had noted the success of a couple of real estate gurus who were touring and speaking on tax liens, and he wanted a tax lien program for Trump University.

He had me interview one applicant, a man named George, who was supposed to be an expert on tax liens. He was already touring and teaching courses. I interviewed George for a couple of hours and thought, "Holy shit, if we hire this man, we're all going to jail."

I told Sexton not to even think about doing business with him. But Sexton was reluctant to let go of someone who could potentially bring in sales. He asked me whether I would give him a trial run, joining him to do a show on tax liens and tax deeds.

"Hell, no!" I said.

I thought that Sexton took my advice and rejected him. But apparently he was already doing Trump University seminars. On August 8, 2008, someone named Mlmguru posted a complaint against Trump University on the Ripoff Report website. This person wrote, "The presenter guy, George, says he was mentored by 'rich uncle' and conveniently his first profit deal was for $50,000. The guy's a New York real estate broker, foreclosure vulture, and most disgustingly, he admitted to being a professional auctioneer and said lots of people get suckered into buying worthless property at auction, and when they can't pay the down payment they get to keep the money."

Trump University also flew me around the country to run field mentorship programs. My bus tours became wildly successful. I treated these three-day sessions like boot camps. I liked to say that if you're going to spend all this money, then you'd better be ready to hit the road at eight in the morning and see twenty-five properties every day. I told people that I didn't care if we had to work until two in the morning. You will get your money's worth. You will be educated.

We would go all day and night, until the students begged me to stop. Students were pleased. I asked one woman who had a lot of energy why she chose me for her field mentorship. She replied, "Because I heard that you're the drill sergeant in real estate. You know what you're doing, but I'd better be prepared to hit the ground running."

One day, after being on the road for several hours looking at houses, she asked, "Are we going to stop to eat?"

"Well, no, not really," I replied. "We've got properties to do. I told you to pack a snack bag."

She said, "Oh, I've got one! I've been eating almonds all morning. I've been eating. I was just waiting for *you* to start eating. I'm just worried about you passing out on me."

I wasn't stopping to eat. I would just go on coffee and oatmeal cookies all day. Later, she said, "Could you do me a favor? I'm a little older than you, and I need more frequent bathroom stops. Can we stop?"

"Of course we'll stop, but you've got to tell me when," I replied. "We have so many properties to see that it's going to take time out of our day."

"You know what?" she said. "Just pull over here at the pharmacy. Wait for me here. Have a coffee and a cigarette. I'll be right out." For the rest of the day, and it was a very long day, she didn't ask to stop at all. She didn't need any more bathroom breaks.

We met later and she gave me rave reviews. She made a lot of money in real estate and she still practices today. She approached me and thanked me for inspiring her and taking her out on that field mentorship.

Then she said, "I've got to tell you a secret."

"What's that?" I asked.

"Remember how I didn't have to go to the bathroom anymore that day? I went into the pharmacy and bought adult diapers. I didn't want to stop the deal flow. I was so excited to make money. And every time that you stopped for coffee, I changed the diaper." I laughed so hard that I almost fell on the ground. I couldn't believe it. I'm so proud of the students of mine who have been successful.

My field mentorships were so well received that word trickled up the grapevine to Donald Trump himself, and for the very first time, he reached out to me. Donald Trump's secretary called and told me that Mr. Trump would like to send me an autographed photograph. She asked for my address. When I received the photo, it was bordered in gold and said, "Awesome job, Steve. Congratulations. Keep up the excellent work."

Being a meek person who was not used to praise, I was thrilled. In hindsight, it was odd that Donald Trump wouldn't have called me personally, and that his secretary would have to ask for my address, since I worked in his office building and he cut my checks. And it speaks volumes about the Trump Organization that the reward for an overperforming employee was a mere signed photograph. I wonder whether he even signed it personally, or if the autopen did it.

Despite my pride in helping thousands of students, many of whom I am still in contact with today, I was only able to impact a fraction of the hundreds of thousands of students who came through Trump University. While some flourished and became millionaires, others I could tell right away didn't have the concentration or focus to be a success. For example, they couldn't handle the mathematical calculations, or they'd have so much anxiety that they couldn't follow through on a purchase that was a good deal. My heart went out to such people and I refused to just take their money. Instead I advised them to get a refund and discontinue personal coaching. Some people had been sold on a dream. When you pay $34,995 for special coaching, it's such an extravagant amount that the only way to justify it to yourself is to believe that you'll get a substantial return on your investment. Students could be very self-delusional about this.

Donald Trump didn't get rich on his own. He was born wealthy, and he was groomed for success. He said he got started with a "small" loan of one million dollars from his father, and insisted that was the whole story. But the *Wall Street Journal* tracked down a 1985 casino-license disclosure that showed Trump's father lent him $14 million—$31 million in today's dollars. And in 1991, New Jersey regulators came after Trump after his father bailed out his failing Trump Castle Casino by buying $3.5 million in chips and never playing them. Trump Castle got to keep the money, but under terms of the settlement, the casino was forced to pay a fine of thirty thousand dollars. Now that was a sweet deal—receive a gift of $3.5 million, for which you must pay a fee of just thirty thousand dollars! By purchasing chips like a regular customer instead of simply giving his son three and a half million bucks, Fred Trump also saved big on the federal gift tax. If my students had that kind of banker sitting at their elbow, they all could have gotten rich in real estate.

Human psychology being what it is, given the choice between accepting that they had been duped into wasting their money, or believing that they could be the next Donald Trump, most students obviously preferred the latter option. So it took quite a bit of work sometimes to get students who were doomed to fail in real estate to admit defeat and move on.

As for the Trump University leadership, my feeling at the time wasn't so much that Michael Sexton was blocking my attempts to fix Trump University, it was more that he had given up. With the ship going down, instead of fixing it, he was just biding his time so that he could step into the lifeboat and row to shore.

I still believe, absolutely, that Trump University could have been fixed. We could have told Trump—who owned roughly ninety-three percent of the school—"We paid off your investment plus millions in profit. You made a lot of money. Now let us reorganize, restructure our business model, get rid of the bad mentors, give out a lot of refunds, and upgrade what we teach." We would have needed another infusion of cash from Donald Trump, but it could have been done.

We could have gone legit. But I was slowly figuring out that I was the only person who wanted to go legit and who was driven by the passion to educate students for real.

Meanwhile, the Trump University ship continued to sink. First, we stopped teaching seminars in Texas, and then in Delaware. In 2010, Greg Abbott, the attorney general of Texas, launched an investigation after the school racked up thirty complaints over two years. We pulled out of the state before the probe was completed. A few years later, Trump made two contributions to Abbott's gubernatorial campaign—one for twenty-five thousand dollars in July 2013 and the other for ten thousand dollars in May 2014. It was Trump's only substantial venture into Texas politics. The governor's critics in the state Democratic Party said that Abbott was "on the corrupt Trump payroll." A former deputy chief of Abbott's consumer protection division, John Owens, claimed that his bosses torpedoed their request to sue Trump University for illegal business practices. A memo dated May 11, 2010, and provided to the *Texas Tribune* and other news organizations, revealed that Owens and his colleagues wanted to ask Trump University for a $5.4 million settlement. In 2016, Owens charged that Republican Texas Attorney General Ken Paxton issued a cease and desist letter to him after he made public copies of a fourteen-page internal summary of the state's case against Donald Trump, accusing him of scamming millions from students of Trump University. Owens, now retired, said his team had built a solid case against Donald Trump and Trump University, but was told to drop it after the school agreed to cease operations in Texas. The former state regulator told the Associated Press that the decision was "highly unusual," leaving the bilked students on their own to attempt to recover their tuition money from the school.

"It was swept under the rug, and the consumers were left with no one to go to bat for them," Owens told the *Texas Tribune*. No one has yet uncovered a smoking gun, but many people think that thirty-five thousand dollars in campaign contributions was a mighty low price for Trump to pay, letting him cut his losses and avoid tangling with Texas lawmen.

Delaware and many other US states have laws that protect distressed homeowners, which say that if you offer a lowball cash deal to convince them to sign over their deed to you, you will go to jail. It's considered predatory, because someone who has no money for food can get taken advantage of very easily by a "rescuer" who steps in with a cash offer that is unethically below the value of the property they want to buy. You'll find horror stories in the news about older people or impoverished people who have had their property essentially stolen from them. And yet Trump University mentors were teaching "cash-for-keys" transactions for quick turnaround sales in states like Delaware where it was banned.

It was completely unethical, and I was horrified. In fact, some of the mentors had to eventually change their names so that they could continue teaching real estate.

17.

On June 2, 2010, Trump University itself announced that it was changing its name to the Trump Entrepreneur Initiative. Everyone assumed the name change was due to the continued demands by the New York State Education Department that the company stop using the word "university" in its name.

This name change had been a long time coming. But that's how Trump operates: the only way to get his attention is to keep hammering him until he decides the cost isn't worth it. That's what it's all about—cost versus benefit, in terms of dollars. Nothing else matters.

In a letter dated May 27, 2005—exactly four days after Trump and Sexton had presided over the school's gala opening press conference in the gilded lobby of Trump Tower—the New York State Department of Education (NYSED) had sharply notified Donald Trump, Michael Sexton, and Trump University that they were violating the New York Education Law by using the word "university" when the school was not actually chartered as one. The NYSED also charged that Trump University was violating the education law because it lacked a license to offer student instruction or training in New York State.

Various terms are used for educational institutions in the United States. The word "school" describes any place where people learn something. A school can teach anything from accounting to needlepoint to surviving in the wilderness. Anyone can take a course at a school.

A "college" provides post-secondary education, and you need a high school diploma to enter a college. A "university" is a group of schools which offer education after secondary school, at least one of which must be a college where students receive a bachelor's degree. The other schools in a university are graduate schools where students receive advanced degrees. Unlike a real college or university, a high school diploma was not required for "admission" to Trump University. The only thing necessary for admission was a valid credit card.

There's no legal restriction on the use of the word "school," and I'm sure that if Trump and Sexton had been less grandiose in their thinking, they could have called the company "Trump Business School" or "Trump School of Real Estate" or even just merely "Trump School." As a for-profit school, they would have needed to apply for a license from the NYSED Bureau of Proprietary School Supervision (BPSS). As the City of New York's "Private School License" webpage says, "Non-degree granting post-secondary schools that operate for profit—such as schools offering vocational training or English as a Second Language (ESL) programs—need licensing from the NYS Department of Education's Bureau of Proprietary School Supervision (BPSS). Proprietary schools under BPSS jurisdiction include trade schools, computer training facilities, and for-profit English as a Second Language (ESL) schools, among others. The Bureau of Proprietary School Supervision requires several licenses to open or operate any for-profit school."

But Donald Trump would never call his enterprise a mere "school" and, like a peasant, apply for a license. Such things were petty annoyances, suitable only for little people. Instead, he called it Trump University, and in his fevered imagination he immediately saw it as being on a par with Harvard, but without the fuss and bother of conforming to either the law or academic tradition. However, once you open a school and brazenly call it a "college" or "university," the state government has a duty to ensure that the school you've organized meets stringent state requirements.

The law is clear. The NYSED website says, "Use of the terms 'college' and 'university' in New York State is generally restricted to institutions chartered by the Regents or the State Legislature. To establish a college or university in New York State, an entity must be authorized by the Board of Regents or its charter to confer degrees. In addition, the Education Department must register every curriculum (program) creditable toward a degree at a New York college or university before the institution may offer the program."

The NYSED recommended a remedy for Trump University. Joseph Frey, assistant commissioner of the Office of Quality Assurance, told Sexton in an email that Trump University would not be subject to the New York license requirement if it had no physical presence in New York State, if they moved the business organization outside of the state, and if they ceased running live programs in the state.

Sexton promptly informed the NYSED that Trump University would merge its operation into a new Delaware LLC, and would indeed cease holding live programming in New York State. However, according to accusations appearing in Cohen v. Trump, not only did Trump University ignore the letter from the NYSED, but "defendant's agents" sought to deceive the NYSED by creating a fictitious Trump University office in Dover, Delaware. Indeed, Trump did create a new LLC at 60 Greentree Drive, Suite 101, Dover, Delaware 19904, but it was nothing more than a mail drop.

High in its luxurious offices at 40 Wall Street in Manhattan, Trump University continued to go about its business as if the NYSED didn't exist. In late 2006 and early 2007, in a further snub to the NYSED, live events were actually *expanded*, both in the state of New York and nationally.

Despite Sexton's misrepresentations to the attorney general, in 2009, through newspaper advertisements and a student complaint to the New York State Attorney General, the NYSED learned that Trump University was continuing to provide live programming and instruction in New York without obtaining proper licensing or moving its operations out of New York. This was not a trivial issue. The New York attorney general argued that the very fact that Trump University LLC was organized and based in New York misled customers into believing Trump University was in compliance with New York laws requiring the licensure, regulation, and chartering of all educational institutions operating within the state. Indeed, Trump University reinforced the lie that it was a real university by flouting many of the signs and symbols of legitimate colleges and universities, and by referring to Trump University speakers as "faculty" and customers as "students" who "graduated" from a completed course. The Trump University course of study was referred to as a "curriculum," and payments were "tuition." Some instructors even claimed that a Trump certificate was "a bit of a college degree" and that Trump University offered "graduate programs, post graduate programs, doctorate programs." This coming from a "school" where many members of the "faculty" were not college educated.

In March 2010, the NYSED sent Trump University another letter demanding that it cease using the word "university" in its name. This time—perhaps because the terminally ill school was gasping on life support and ready to be trucked off to the morgue—Trump University complied, at least in part. In fact, the school sent a cheery email to their students:

"To celebrate our increased commitment to meet your growing entrepreneurial needs, we are pleased to announce that Trump University has officially changed its name to the Trump Entrepreneur Initiative. This change reflects our ongoing mission to empower you—the next generation of entrepreneurs, business builders, and investors—with the tools and confidence to achieve your personal and financial goals... We have worked hard to earn your trust and take great pride in our exceptional 98% Student Satisfaction Rating. Our commitment to your success is stronger than ever!"

According to a 2013 deposition, Michael Sexton said that his final day of work was July 31, 2010. Maybe he was telling the truth, but the last time I saw him at work he was wearing a natty wool blazer. It was at the end of a usual workday at 40 Wall Street. The vibe in the office was strange, because employees had been gradually leaving and had not been replaced. Eventually the staff dwindled to a skeleton crew of just four people: myself, Mark Covais (who had become director of operations), Paul Reisner, and Diego Guevera.

Michael Sexton came into our office on the thirty-second floor and, with his attaché case in his hand, and he gave us a cheery wave. "See you guys tomorrow," he said. Then he went to the elevator and rode down to his waiting Jaguar. The next morning, he didn't come to the office.

This was not unusual, because he was often absent. But as the days and weeks passed with no sign of our boss—whom we respected and whom we were trying to serve to the best of our abilities—we started to become curious. One day I said, "Guys, let's just go into his office and see what's going on."

This was a brazen plan, because *no one* just walked into Sexton's office. It was like a holy temple. But we were getting desperate, so we boldly opened the door and went in. It looked like he had just stepped out for coffee. His desk was covered with the usual papers and reports. Nothing was out of place. He could have walked in, sat down, and picked up where he left off. We stood there for a moment, dumbfounded. With a shrug, we left, and I closed the door behind us.

What the name change really meant was that we were done. In reality, Michael Sexton had shut Trump University down without telling the staff that the company was finished. Sexton frequently traveled away from the office, so it took us weeks to figure out that our jobs had evaporated. I never did get my last paycheck. No one ever told us to stop coming into work.

In August and September 2010, the NYSED once again informed Trump University that the company needed a license to operate, which it still lacked despite having been notified in 2005 that its failure to obtain a license violated New York State law. Finally, on October 7, 2010, Michael Sexton notified the NYSED that Trump University had ceased operations.

The Trump Entrepreneur Institute is still currently a viable legal entity. Donald Trump has even said that someday he intends to resurrect Trump University from the grave and, like a crazed zombie terrorizing a village, turn it loose among the population. On June 2, 2016 he tweeted: "After the litigation is disposed of and the case won, I have instructed my execs to open Trump U(?), so much interest in it! I will be pres." He also said that his children—Eric, Don Jr., and Ivanka—would run the school on his behalf. "We have a lot of great people who want to get back into Trump University," he told his cheering supporters at an election rally.

18.

One of my last encounters with a Trump University official was particularly bizarre. It was a few weeks after we had last seen Michael Sexton. At 40 Wall Street, the remaining staff and I were dutifully answering the phones and trying our best to assist angry and bitter students.

Suddenly we were summoned to Trump Tower on Fifth Avenue. This was like being called from your peasant's hovel to make the journey to the king's castle, where you'd be admitted to the highest and most regal throne room. Six of us—myself, Mark Covais, Diego Guevera, Paul Reisner and two customer service reps—hurried uptown to 725 Fifth Avenue and walked through the imposing doors of Trump's opulent headquarters. We felt so special that we even paused to have our photo taken in the famous lobby. What could they want from us? I know they hadn't summoned us to fire us, because if Sexton wanted to get rid of us he'd just send us an email. It had to be something big that required our presence. Were we going to go legit?

We were admitted to a conference room covered in soft white marble. It looked like an expensive mausoleum. We sat down at the table. At the center of the table was the usual triangular space-ship-looking conference call unit. Trump's lawyer Michael Cohen came into the room. My heart froze. This was not good.

Michael Cohen, who was known around the office as "Pitbull," was executive vice president of the Trump Organization and special counsel to Donald Trump. Born and raised on Long Island, he had graduated from American University and the Thomas M. Cooley Law School. He started his career as a liberal Democrat, volunteering for the 1988 presidential campaign of Michael Dukakis. He was even a legislative intern for Democratic congressman Joe Moakley. But like his boss, he drifted into the Republican Party, running for New York City Council in 2003 as a Republican before briefly campaigning for a seat in the New York State Senate in 2010.

On that day in the summer of 2011, Michael Cohen—Pitbull—stood at the end of the table, glaring at us. I sat there quietly, trying to look cool but respectful. Skipping any pleasantries, Cohen immediately launched into a bitter tirade.

"I want to know where the money has been going!" he barked. "Somebody knows what's going on. Somebody has been stealing from Trump University and from Mr. Trump. You're going to tell me who."

We were thunderstruck. What the hell? We weren't the accountants! "What do you mean?" I replied as calmly as I could.

"There's a problem," he snarled at me. "Money is *missing*. It's going somewhere. I intend to find out where. Tell me *now*."

"Don't look at me," I replied. "I have nothing to do with what happens to the money. My job is to try to keep our students from suing us for fraud. I'm trying to help this company *keep* its money! That's what each of us does, every day!"

I suppose he thought I was lying—which was ridiculous because I didn't handle Trump University funds. After a few minutes of back-and-forth, he exploded, "Gilpin, what the fuck do you know? I'll make sure you never fuck your spouse again! Got it?"

To this bizarre rant I calmly replied, using the same measured voice that my father had used on me, "Mr. Cohen, my spouse passed away a year ago." It was true. I didn't share much of my private life with people at work, but my spouse had in fact passed away from cancer the previous year. I added, "I hope I don't ever fuck my dead spouse."

At that moment a disembodied voice came from the triangular conference call unit. "Mr. Cohen, please come to my office. *Immediately!*"

It was the voice of Donald Trump. One of my associates sitting at the table started laughing uncontrollably. "Pitbull" backed off like a lamb. White as a sheet, Cohen hurriedly left the room. I was astounded. Had Donald Trump been silently listening to our conversation? As soon as the door closed, I burst out laughing, too. It was all just so bizarre!

What a fool Cohen had been, I thought as we got up from the table and filed out the door. If you want to get information from somebody, why on earth would you start off by barking at them? Cohen was a smart guy and a tough lawyer. But for some reason he believed that the best way to get someone to see a problem from your point of view was to bite them in the leg.

It didn't work with me, nor did it work with anyone on our team at 40 Wall Street. It was doubly offensive because we were the only ones left on the front lines who were trying to protect the good name of Donald J. Trump. His idea of showing gratitude was to haul us in and accuse us of stealing.

As to whether or not Trump was eavesdropping, it was certainly possible. On June 30, 2016 *Buzzfeed* published allegations that Trump eavesdropped on employee phone calls at Mar-a-Lago, his luxury Palm Beach resort that he ran as a club for paying guests and celebrities. Among the staff, it was common knowledge that in the bedroom of his private suite, Trump had a telephone console installed that acted like a switchboard, connecting to every phone extension on the estate. Mar-a-Lago had a common type of company phone network with a "barge-in" capability, which allowed certain users to tap into and discreetly monitor other calls in the network. Several employees told BuzzFeed that Trump used the console to eavesdrop on calls involving staff. They said that Trump listened in on phone calls at the club during the mid-2000s, though they did not know if he had eavesdropped more recently.

The source recalled an incident when a staff member was on the phone with a club member. During the phone call, Trump called the staff member on another line and made a comment on the very issue that was being discussed. "There is no other way you could know what that conversation was about unless you were eavesdropping," the source said. Trump campaign spokeswoman Hope Hicks denied the story, telling *BuzzFeed*, "This is totally and completely untrue."

When it comes to privacy, Trump tends to be paranoid—or perhaps just realistic—once telling conservative radio host Hugh Hewitt, "I tend to err on the side of security . . . . I assume when

I pick up my telephone people are listening to my conversations anyway, if you want to know the truth."

With the rest of the group, I returned to my office at 40 Wall Street. I never heard anything more from Michael Cohen.

The truth was, I had really looked up to Michel Sexton. I thought he was a bright guy who could have built Trump University into something that could truly educate and inspire people all over America. It could have been legitimate—after all, say what you will about Donald Trump, but he's got a unique brilliance for making money in real estate. With guidance from Sexton, Trump could have built another kind of monument to himself—a positive legacy of helping ordinary people make money from real estate investments. To me, it seemed they both chose to go for the quick buck and the tawdry scam. It was really a shame.

Around Christmas of 2011, I said goodbye to the remaining staff, including Mark Covais, who as of this writing remains the director of operations of the Trump Entrepreneur Initiative. I left the office on the thirty-second floor of 40 Wall Street and never went back to work there again.

As the months passed, I felt as if I were slowly crawling out from under the shadow of Donald Trump. On the outside, I could see the totality of the Trump University disaster so much more clearly. I was proud to have helped thousands of students, but there was no way that I could have fixed Trump University's underperformance, because the fraud was a deliberate push to wring money from gullible students. Management didn't want to teach real estate. They used me as a shield. I was the one expert who was doing actual work at Trump University and my existence there gave cover to others who were acting unethically and predatorily. In some cases I could rescue students and serve them well, but most of the time, their problems seemed impossible to unravel.

As for Donald Trump, he did what he does: he made money and got away with it. Michael Sexton testified that over the course of five years, 80,308 people attended the free Preview events, 9,208 attended the three-day workshops at $1,495 each (though it's not clear how many were discounted or came as guests), and 794 people purchased Elite-level mentorships.

Mark Covais testified that around six thousand people paid between $995 and $1,995 to attend three-day seminars, and 572 people paid the full $34,995 for the top- level Trump Gold Elite mentorship. While we don't know for sure, let's hypothesize that the 794 Elite-level students each paid an average of twenty thousand dollars. That alone would give the company nearly sixteen million dollars in income. To that, you can add the roughly nine million dollars earned by the three-day workshops, as well as the revenue from the sales of books and CDs.

After deducting operating expenses—the fees for the staff, presenters, hotels, and advertising— ninety percent of the profits went straight into the piggy bank of Donald J. Trump. Former Trump University Controller Steven Matejek said in a deposition that Trump repaid himself the money that he invested, plus "it had to have been five million, or several million" more in capital distributions. The deposition specifically refers to a payment of $1.5 million to Trump. An October 2008 check entered as evidence also shows Trump distributing five hundred thousand dollars to himself.

New York's attorney general said Trump may have pocketed as much as five million dollars from Trump University. Donald Trump, the man at the center of the whirlwind, has been vague on how much he made from the company; he's said it's "a million, or more." And Trump's lawyers have acknowledged the billionaire profited from Trump University, but not how much.

At a 2016 election rally in South Carolina, he said he "would have given all the money to charity" had he not been sued. However, the fact was that he wasn't sued until the school was already in its death throes.

It's possible that Trump, Sexton, and the other top brass may have thought that, like Trump Airlines or Trump Vodka, Trump University would fade quietly into the misty pages of history. They probably hoped that the suckers they had bilked would move on with their lives and pay off their credit cards while carrying bitter memories of their brief association with the great Donald Trump, doing nothing about it.

They were very mistaken. The long-term effects of the mistreatment of its students not only remained, but intensified. Instead of being forgotten or written off, the school's crimes were carefully catalogued by our angry students, who one by one, all over the country, sought out lawyers for relief. As the months and years passed, the bitterness of the housewives, retirees, entrepreneurs, and aspiring real estate tycoons who had taken our courses did not ease: instead they increased as they continued to pay huge credit card bills which carried compound interest. You can imagine the feelings of a student who had taken on twenty, thirty, or fifty thousand dollars of debt to purchase a "Trump University" education, only to discover that with few exceptions they have been taught nothing more than they could have learned on Wikipedia for free. No secrets had been revealed, no proprietary Trump insights were learned, no doors were opened. For our students, Donald Trump had been nothing more than a giant gilded face glaring down from the towering posters at the front of the lecture halls, or a golden signature autopenned on a worthless Trump University certificate which was handed to you only after you had provided a glowing review, like a prisoner in North Korea happy to videotape a confession before being granted release. It didn't take long for the students who felt cheated and deceived to organize themselves.

19.

On April 30, 2010, in US District Court for Southern California, the firm of Robbins Geller Rudman & Dowd, LLP, along with the law firm of Zeldes & Haeggquist, LLP, filed the first nationwide class action lawsuit against Trump University on behalf of consumers who were duped into purchasing Trump University real estate investing seminars.

The lead plaintiff was Tarla Makaeff, a Los Angeles yoga and Pilates instructor who had paid nearly sixty thousand dollars to Trump University in 2008. This was the same Tarla Makaeff who had written positive reviews and had appeared on a video, filmed at the conclusion of a workshop in a hotel ballroom, in which she cheerfully praised her mentor, Troy Peterson, as well as the speaker, Omar Peru.

When she made her effusive video, Makaeff probably didn't know that Troy Peterson had come to Trump University from a company called Dynetech, where he had been an "executive mentor" from 2003 to 2005. As of October 2016, according to his LinkedIn profile, Peterson said at Dynetech he "worked with entrepreneurs to aid them in business start-up. Program involved basic start-up to advanced strategies for building income and wealth. Included strategies to build and execute an effective business plan, calculating and projecting profit and cost analysis, marketing and management of clients and personnel." In his description, the magic words "real estate" did not appear.

Unfortunately, Dynetech, best known for its "wealth seminars" and investment software, had a dubious reputation and serious problems with state regulators. As the *Orlando Business Journal* reported, in 1996 the state of Tennessee had sued Dynetech, resulting in a settlement involving allegations that Dynetech's so-called Diversified Cash Flow Institute promoted seminars that misrepresented the value and cost of the training. In 2004, a Tennessee administrative judge dismissed a complaint from the Tennessee Securities Division seeking to shut down the company for enticing people to pay $4,995 for seminars that were business investments.

In October 2009, Texas prosecutors accused Dynetech of violating the state's deceptive trade practices and consumer protection law for staging expensive, but misleading, business-training seminars. The suit said Texas investigators had collected responses from hundreds of consumers who believe they were duped, and the company and its subsidiaries specifically "acquired and deprived money or other property from consumers who were sixty-five years of age or older."

The defendants who were named included seminar promoter Fred Steinberg of Boca Raton. The suit said, "Fred Steinberg and his companies have over the years created numerous seminars to 'get rich quick' to the detriment of hundreds of angered and disappointed victims."

That same year, the *Orlando Sentinel* reported that Florida regulators had fielded scores of consumer complaints about Dynetech's how-to-get-rich-quick programs over the years. Since 2003, more than 130 complaints had been filed with the Florida Attorney General's Office via that agency's fraud hotline. But in each case, the office had tagged the complaint as "unregulated" and instead sent it to the state's Department of Agriculture and Consumer Services. No further action had been taken. The paper noted, "The Florida complaints bear a strong resemblance to ones filed in Texas that triggered a deceptive-trade-practices lawsuit by authorities there."

When it filed Chapter 11 bankruptcy in 2009, Dynetech cited debts of more than $14.5 million and potential penalties of $10 billion from the Texas lawsuit. Troy Peterson was one of Donald Trump's "hand-picked" mentors who were supposed to take students and personally show them how to legally buy and sell real estate at a profit. It's no wonder that, like thousands of other customers, when the truth was revealed to her, Tarla Makaeff's enthusiasm for the program quickly soured into bitter regret and anger.

The suit, Makaeff v. Trump University, LLC, sought refunds for Makaeff and for other former clients of Trump University, as well as punitive damages for breach of contract, fraud, negligent misrepresentation, and bad faith. It did not originally name Donald Trump as a defendant, but it did so later in an amended complaint.

Tarla Makaeff was like many other hopeful people who trusted Donald Trump and believed what he claimed in the Trump

University marketing materials. She trusted and believed what his "hand-picked" speakers told her. She trusted the advertisements that featured Donald Trump boasting, "I can turn anyone into a successful real estate investor, including you," enticing students with lines like, "Are *you* my next Apprentice?" and "Learn from my hand-picked experts how you can profit from the largest real estate liquidation in history." In fact, as we'll see later, her experience was not unique, and the fact that her name was at the top of the page did not mean that another victim's name could not be readily substituted.

During the three-day workshop, Makaeff was told to raise her credit card limits four times so she could enter in to "real estate transactions." On August 10 Makaeff put the Gold Elite Program on her credit card. Because she didn't earn a penny trading real estate, the price would ultimately include the variable APR finance charges, interest fees, and late fees she would have to pay her credit card company.

You can go online to any credit card finance calculator and plug in the numbers. Start with a balance of $35,000 at 18% interest. Your first minimum monthly payment will be $875.00, declining gradually from there. It will take you 467 months to be rid of your debt. In that time, you will pay $51,926.36 in interest. The total you will have paid to your credit card company will be nearly eighty-seven thousand dollars.

To finance your Trump Gold Elite package, you could owe eighty-seven thousand dollars paid over a period of thirty-eight years. Remember that real undergraduate student loans from real colleges typically carry an interest rate of five percent, and there are many ways to get generous deferments if you're unemployed or still in school. Credit card companies don't care: like Donald Trump, they just want their money.

Having handed over her credit card, Makaeff was now entitled to four three-day advanced training workshops, a three-day mentoring session in the field, and training publications, software, and other materials. There is a possibility that these might have been worthwhile if these products had actually been delivered.

James Harris immediately told Makaeff that he would now be personally available to her by phone and email, and shortly thereafter emailed to her, "We can do a ton together." She never heard from him again. Instead, she was shunted to another mentor, Tiffany Brinkman, who, Makaeff claims, told her that her first real estate deal would pay off her Trump credit card bill.

Makaeff's enthusiasm for the program, duly recorded in the video in which she praises her mentor Troy Peterson, quickly waned. In April 2009, after completing five more programs and workshops at a cost of approximately sixty thousand dollars, and after seven months of the Gold Elite Program, she called a Trump University representative and complained. She was told that that she was "ineligible" for a refund of the cost of the program. She then sent an email to Trump University complaining that she was in a "precarious financial position" and that she "did not receive the value that I thought I would for such a large expenditure."

Remember, part of the relentless pitch that speakers and mentors made to students was that they'd quickly earn back the fees they paid for the workshops. It was a common ploy used by James Harris and others to ask the prospects to write out a check to themselves for one million dollars and then tape it to their mirror. Soon enough, Harris promised, the student would be able to cash that check.

Instead of offering her a refund, in response to Makaeff's email, Trump University offered more free mentoring services, which Makaeff accepted. Over the next month or so, she was coached into two real estate deals. In the first of her deals, Trump mentor Tad Lignell introduced her to a real estate agent, Noah Herrera of Las Vegas, regarding a property purchase in Las Vegas. Lignell did not disclose to his student that he had a financial interest in referring Trump students to Noah Herrera. The Gold Elite "Power Team" then misquoted comps to Makaeff. Comps, or comparables, are regarded as the single-best tool in determining a home's value. They contrast criteria from recently sold properties in a neighborhood, such as sale price, age of house, size, and square footage. Real estate agents use comps to prepare a comparative market analysis for their clients. Rather than making a profit on the deal, as she would have made if the comps had been correct, she would have likely suffered a loss of twenty percent on the transaction. When she discovered that the comps were incorrect and that she was likely to lose money on the deal, she looked for a way out.

It's alleged that someone fraudulently altered the real estate documents that Makaeff had previously signed at the escrow office without her authorization or approval. As a result of this illegal conduct, Makaeff was permitted to void the transaction, which she did.

The only other real estate transaction that came Makaeff's way involved a Houston property. Fortunately, I was able to steer her away from this particular disaster. As "expert, interactive support," she was provided only a toll-free telephone number to call, and I was the person on the other end of the phone. When Tarla Makaeff called me, I told her that she should *never* accept a deal that did not provide at least one hundred dollars a month in positive cash flow. Anything less was a waste of time and money. The deal she was calling about was referred by a partner named Mike Kasper to another of Makaeff's Trump mentors, Rick McNally, who stood to financially benefit from the deal. This potential sale raised an inherent and improper conflict of interest, and would generate only forty dollars a month in positive cash flow. It was one snake doing another snake a favor. Such was the ethos of Trump University. Makaeff wisely rejected this fetid arrangement.

In her lawsuit, Makaeff charged that her Trump University mentors had instructed her to engage in illegal real estate practices, such as posting advertising "bandit signs" on the sides of roadways. Bandit signs are simply cheap signs that advertise anything, but most of them typically say, "We Buy Ugly Houses" or "We Take Your Junk," plus a phone number. Many communities have laws against them. In California they're illegal. This is not some arcane, dusty statute buried in deep in the code of law. It's Real Estate 101. Every competent real estate broker in America knows their state and local laws regarding bandit signs. You might say, "Who cares? What's the big fuss over a bunch of signs? What can they do to you?" In California, however, the authorities can do plenty.

On June 18, 2009, Makaeff received a letter from the Orange County District Attorney's Office informing her that posting bandit signs in California without lawful permission could subject her to fines, a misdemeanor charge, and up to six months in jail.

Trump University argued that it specifically instructed Makaeff to seek local legal counsel to ensure that any signs that she put up would be permissible in her community before she posted them. According to Trump University, notice was given to Makaeff in the form on a handout in a binder provided to her eight or nine months before she posted the signs. The form stated, "Make sure you check with the city first because you could have your signs removed or a potential fine." But which do you think carries more weight with a student—an obscure handout in a binder, or your "hand-picked" Trump University mentor saying, "I'm telling you, this is what you need to do."

It seems as though Trump salespeople not only urged their students to get their credit limits raised on their existing cards, but they may have fraudulently procured new credit cards in their students' names. Makaeff also charged that in 2008 someone at Trump University provided her personal financial information to HSBC Bank and opened a credit card on Makaeff's behalf without her authorization. During a phone interview with a Trump University coaching representative, Makaeff was told that she was pre-approved for an HSBC/Prosper Learning credit card. Makaeff testified that she believed that because HSBC had sufficient information to pre-approve her for a credit card, Trump University had provided Makaeff's personal and financial information to HSBC without Makaeff's authorization.

By autumn 2009, the relationship between Makaeff and Trump University had disintegrated. Makaeff wrote to her bank and the Better Business Bureau, contacted government agencies, and posted on Internet message boards about her dispute with Trump

University. Makaeff requested a refund of $5,100 from her bank for services charged for Trump University programs. In the letter to the Better Business Bureau, Makaeff requested a refund of her payments for services that she did not receive. Here's one of her complaints:

> I am contacting the Better Business Bureau (BBB), the Federal Trade Commission (FTC), Bureau of Consumer Protection and the FDIC as well as posting the facts of my highly negative experience on a wide variety of Internet sites to ensure that this organization at some point is stopped from defrauding others with its predatory behavior. I am also contacting the media to give them a statement of facts so that they can expose this scam and am willing to go to whatever lengths necessary to obtain my money back including taking legal action at the state and federal levels for this crime that has been committed to thousands of students nationwide who have been preyed on and victimized as I know I am one of many.

On September 10, 2009, Makaeff sent a four-page letter to Bank of America, her credit card company, complaining about Trump University and requesting a refund of the money she spent on Trump University programs. In this letter, Makaeff accused Trump University of engaging in, among other wrongs: (1) grand larceny; (2) identify theft; (4) attempting to trick her into opening lines of credit without her approval. Specifically, Makaeff stated:

> I want to make you aware that the HSBC bank has separated from any relation with any Trump University, Trump

Institute, Trump subsidiaries such as Prosper Inc., and any party related to the aforementioned because of cases such as mine in which the aforementioned companies participated in the dispersal of my personal financial information and opening of credit between a multitude of entitles including banks regulated by the FDIC. This type of fraudulent sales techniques are governed by state and federal protection consumers such as me against this outright Fraud, Grand Larceny, and Identity Theft by Trump University/ Profit Publishing Group.

I was tricked into signing up for this when my information was taken under high pressure sales tactics clearly in violation of state and federal statutes protecting consumers from high pressure sales tactics, bait and switch, unsolicited taking of personal credit, and trickery into opening credit cards without *my* approval or understanding.

Tarla Makaeff included my name in her complaint. One of the other plaintiffs mentioned me also. On or about October 20, 2009, a student named John Brown talked to Trump University's Jason Schauer about his concerns that he would actually get what he was promised, and whether it was prudent to pay for this program based on his financial situation. Like the typical hard-sell salesman, Schauer reassured him and urged him to make the purchase.

Brown called Schauer again on October 29, 2009, and told him he was concerned that after his three-day mentorship he would be left to fend for himself, and that charging twenty-five thousand dollars for the program on his two credit cards would financially max him out, leaving him no money to invest in real estate.

The obvious logic says that if you're twenty-five thousand dollars in debt and have no more access to credit or cash, *you're not going to be buying a building.* However, Schauer assured Brown that he would receive a full-year of one-on-one mentoring in real estate investing.

For twenty-five thousand dollars, Brown did not receive a seminar. He only received mentoring—and he received it from me. I had several phone conversations with John Brown, and I'm not at all surprised that he stated in his complaint that our conversations "were not useful or helpful." I had no time to offer anything of substance to Brown, other than to ask him if he had any questions and to try to answer them as best as I could.

On or about December 17, 2009, Brown called Trump University to complain, stating that he was frustrated with the mentoring he was receiving and that I did not have time for him because of all of the other students I was mentoring.

Sadly, it was true. There was no conceivable way that I could provide full value to the hundreds of students who were calling me. I was like one of those doctors who appear on syndicated radio programs, taking calls from listeners. You've got to give each caller a few minutes and then move on because the phone lines are lit up like a Christmas tree.

I knew the Trump mentality first hand, and I knew how they would respond to the Makaeff lawsuit. I could easily imagine that within the golden chambers of the mighty Trump Organization high in Trump Tower fists pounded on desks and angry voices made bitter demands that this *peasant* be swiftly and decisively *crushed.*

"Tarla who?"

"Makaeff, sir."

"Who the hell is she?"

"One of our Trump University students, sir. A yoga instructor in California." "And she's *suing* me?"

"Yes, sir."

"Is she *crazy*? Doesn't she know who she's up against?"

"She has a big law firm behind her, sir. Robbins Geller Rudman & Dowd. They got a settlement from Enron of over seven billion dollars. They're heavyweights."

"Yeah? Well, screw them. No one gets a penny from me. No one. We will ruin her."

True to form, Trump responded swiftly to the class action lawsuit. On May 26, 2010 Trump filed a counterclaim alleging Makaeff had made defamatory statements about the company, "including many completely spurious accusations of actual crimes," that had somehow caused Trump University losses of more than one million dollars.

The Trump counterclaim attempted to rebut all of Makaeff's claims. For example, as for Makaeff's failure to protest Trump University's opening of a credit card for her in 2008, Trump University claimed that Makaeff "knew in 2008 . . . that a credit card was being opened for her, she consented to it being opened, and agreed to charging the Profit courses on the new card." Trump University further argued that Makaeff did not immediately contact her banks or credit card companies, did not cancel the credit card, and did not even hang up the phone when she found out the credit card had been opened. According to Trump University, it was not until Makaeff tried to get her money back that Makaeff "concocted a story of wrongdoing" regarding the credit card.

On June 30, Makaeff's lawyers countered that Trump University's defamation claim was a "strategic lawsuit against public participation," known as a SLAPP suit. A SLAPP suit is defined as a lawsuit that masquerades as an ordinary lawsuit but is brought to deter common citizens from exercising their political or legal rights, and to intimidate them into withdrawing. Makaeff's lawyers added that because Trump University itself was a "public figure," the defamation claim required proof that she "acted with actual malice" when speaking and writing about Trump University. To prove actual malice, a defamation plaintiff must show by clear and convincing evidence that the defendant knew her statements were false at the time she made them, or that she acted with reckless disregard of the truth or falsity of the statements made.

Eventually, U.S. District Judge Gonzalo P. Curiel ruled in Makaeff's favor and dismissed Trump's defamation claim, ordering Trump University to reimburse Makaeff $798,000 in legal fees and costs. On March 8, 2016, PBS Newshour reported that Tarla Makaeff had "had enough of Donald Trump after spending six years fighting him in court," and asked the court to withdraw from the suit. Her lawyers said that Trump—who by that time was the front-runner in the Republican presidential primary—and his team had put her "through the wringer" and made the prospect of a trial unbearable.

Trump's attorneys insisted that if Makaeff were allowed to withdraw, then the lawsuit should be dismissed altogether, arguing that their trial strategy centered on her. They had deposed her four times and identified her as "the critical witness" in a court filing.

Makaeff's attorneys responded that Trump's argument that their client was indispensable to the billionaire's defense was "illogical to the point of being nearly incomprehensible." They noted that the judge had allowed two plaintiffs to withdraw the previous year, while three others would remain.

"The reason they want her out of the case is she is a horrible, horrible witness," said Trump at a campaign rally in Arkansas. "She's got in writing that she loves it. And I could have settled it and when I saw her documentation . . . Why would I give her money? Probably should have settled it, but I just can't do that. Mentally I can't do it. I'd rather spend a lot more money and fight it."

Makaeff didn't imagine that she would be subjected to criticism under the glare of a presidential campaign, her attorneys said. She had been deposed for a total of nearly sixteen hours and suffered anxiety about finances while Trump sued her for defamation.

"Understandably, Makaeff wants her life back without living in fear of being disparaged by Trump on national television," they wrote in a court filing. In a statement to the court, Makaeff said she was also grieving her mother's death. "I am very concerned about the toll that the trial would take on my emotional and physical health and well-being," she wrote.

On March 21, 2016, over objections from the attorneys for Trump University, Judge Gonzalo Curiel allowed Makaeff to withdraw as the lead plaintiff, naming Sonny Low in her stead, resulting in the new case title Low v. Trump University, LLC.

In June, on the campaign trail, Donald Trump attacked Judge Curiel, who he charged had "an absolute conflict" in presiding over the litigation given that he was "of Mexican heritage" and a member of a Latino lawyers' association. Trump said the background of the judge, who was born in Indiana to Mexican immigrants, was relevant because of his campaign stance against illegal immigration and his pledge to seal the southern U.S. border. "I'm building a wall. It's an inherent conflict of interest," said Trump. Judge Curiel, in adherence to the strict code of ethics followed by judges, made no comment.

20.

On October 18, 2013, Trump University was slammed with another class action lawsuit. Brought by the same two California law firms as the Makaeff suit—Robbins Gellar Rudman & Dowd LLP and Zeldes Haeggquist & Eck LLP—the Cohen lawsuit was nationwide in its scope, whereas the Makaeff lawsuit only included California, Florida, and New York. The complaints were much the same: students had been pressured into buying expensive education packages that, in their opinion, were worthless.

Art Cohen, the lead plaintiff, was a businessman and resident of the state of California. Cohen said he learned about Trump University in 2009 when he saw an advertisement in the *San Jose Mercury News*, to which he subscribed. He also received by mail a "special invitation" to Trump University from Donald Trump, which included two VIP tickets to the free Preview workshop. (How could they be "VIP" tickets if the event was *free* to anyone? Because Trump makes everything sound extra-special even when it is not.) Like thousands of other hopeful students, Cohen was impressed by Donald Trump's name and reputation as a real estate expert and by Trump's assertions that he was personally involved in the education programs. On April 29, 2009, Cohen attended the Preview Live Event at the Fremont Marriott Silicon Valley in Fremont, California. There he viewed what's now called the Main Promotional Video.

The Cohen lawsuit maintained that the Trump University marketing campaign was fueled by the Main Promotional Video, which was published to YouTube so it would be viewed by prospective "student-victims" (as the lawsuit called them) throughout the country. To cast a wide net for customers, Trump University is alleged to have operated an extensive advertising campaign with an annual budget at one time of $6 million and a database of over one million current and potential customers, which it targeted with frequent email blasts.

Based on the speaker's lies that students would receive Donald Trump's real estate secrets from his two handpicked "professors" and mentors at Trump University, Cohen purchased the $1,495 Fast Track to Foreclosure Real Estate Retreat, which he attended from May 8-10, 2009, at the Sheraton Palo Alto Hotel in Palo Alto. At the three-day event, Cohen was upsold to the Trump Gold Elite program, which he purchased on May 10, 2009 for $34,995, plus the interest and finance charges paid to his credit card.

After a thorough analysis of the promises made repeatedly in Trump marketing materials and sales scripts, the lawsuit summed up the scam very succinctly: "Defendant knew that these representations were false, that Defendant Trump was not actively involved in Trump University's Live Events and did not select or interview Trump University's Live Event instructors or mentors, that Defendant Trump offered no input into the actual instruction provided to Trump University's student-victims, that a ghost writer wrote the Donald Trump blogs and wrote most or all of the answers to the 'Ask Donald Trump' questions, and that Trump University did not have a faculty of professors and adjunct professors, but rather independent contractors paid commissions for sales. In other words, Defendant promised Trump University, but delivered neither Donald Trump nor a University."

The Cohen lawsuit also charged that in devising and executing the scheme, Donald Trump and Trump University personnel violated the Racketeer Influenced and Corrupt Organizations Act ("RICO") by devising and knowingly carrying out a "material scheme artifice to defraud or to obtain money by means of materially false or fraudulent pretenses, representations, promises, or omissions of material facts." Trump University used thousands of mail and interstate wire communications to create and perpetuate the scheme through misrepresentations, concealments, and material omissions.

Basically, what the lawsuit charged was that Trump University's fundamental marketing message—that Donald Trump was personally involved the education of Trump University students—was not merely a commonplace advertising exaggeration ("Fewer wrinkles in thirty days or your money back!") but a deliberate act of *criminal fraud*.

With this focus, the Cohen action differed from Makaeff. While the Makaeff action focused on the quality of the product delivered (or not delivered) to the student, Cohen's emphasis was on the misrepresentation of Donald Trump's personal involvement, and the subsequent scheme to make money based on that specific misrepresentation.

Thursday, December 10, 2015, was an exceptionally warm day in Manhattan. When the temperature reached sixty degrees, pedestrians on Fifth Avenue walked coatless, asking each other if the unusual East Coast warm spell was a symptom of global warming. There was talk of a balmy and snowless Christmas, and how it would be tough on the guys who had to wear those hot Santa Claus costumes and scratchy fake beards. High in Trump Tower, in one of the cool marble-clad conference rooms, a legal team from Robbins Geller Rudman & Dowd was taking a video deposition from the defendant, Donald J. Trump on behalf of *Cohen v. Trump*.

Questioning Donald Trump was Jason Forge, a former assistant U.S. attorney who had investigated and prosecuted some of the nation's most significant cases, including the largest corruption case in congressional history.

Representing Donald Trump was Daniel Petrocelli of the firm O'Melveny & Myers in Los Angeles. Some of Petrocelli's other celebrity clients had included Enron CEO Jeffrey Skilling, Fred Goldman in his suit against O.J. Simpson, and Manny Pacquiao in his suit against various boxing notables who had accused Pacquiao of taking performance-enhancing drugs.

During the seven-hour deposition, Forge wanted to determine, among other things, if Donald Trump recognized any of the speakers and mentors that he had supposedly "hand-picked" to serve with Trump University. The logic was that even if six or eight years had elapsed, Trump ought to at least have a familiarity with his Trump University staff.

"Can you identify a single person who was a live events instructor for Trump University?" asked Forge, under the unblinking eye of the video camera.

"You'd have to give me a list," replied Trump. "You'd have to show me the list. I actually went—I would go and just walk in and just stand in the back of the room on occasion just to see how they were doing, but it's been so many years, I wouldn't be able to do that." Trump said he would *stand in the back of the room and watch,* presumably right next to the Easter Bunny and the Lucky Charms leprechaun.

"Let me just give you some names," said Forge, "and you tell me whether this could be a live events instructor, a student, neither."

"Okay," replied Trump gamely. "Johnny Harris," said Forge. "Too many years," said Trump.

While in this first instance Forge asked Trump if he knew "Johnny Harris," a few minutes later he corrected himself and asked Trump repeatedly if he knew James Harris. The answer was always the same: Trump didn't know him and didn't recognize the name.

Was Donald Trump actually saying that he didn't recognize the name of his number one presenter, the guy who pulled in more cash for Trump University than anyone else? There were three possibilities for his answer: 1) Trump had a severe memory problem; 2) he knew James Harris and was lying; or 3) Michael Sexton never discussed *any* of the Trump University personnel during their regular business meetings. Forge put more names before Trump: Tim Gorsline, Mike Dubin, Darren Liebmann, Johnny Burkins, Johnny Horton, Tim Voss.

"Again, you can go through this whole list," complained Trump, "and I'm sure you'd like to so you can take this for a long time, but these are—some of those names sound familiar to me, but it's too many years ago."

"Chris Goff?" asked Forge.

"Are you going to go through a whole list of names?"

"You're the one that said, give me a list."

After more complaining from Trump and lawyering from Petrocelli, Forge continued with the names: Ken Berry, James Webb, James Casper, Mike Casper, Kerry Martin, Paul Lucas, Kerry Lucas, Mike Peterson, Troy Peterson, Chris Gillem. Trump said they sounded familiar, but it had been too many years.

"Steve Gilpin," said Forge.

"Same answer." Familiar, but too many years.

I resented being lumped in with the motivational speakers and con artists who led the workshops. I was the only one of the bunch who was qualified. I gave the Trump University live events their only legitimacy. I was the guy who tried for five years to make Trump University look good. I was the guy who, day after day, talked to the students and tried to cool them off, to defuse their anxiety and anger, to correct the lies they had been told by the "hand-picked" instructors, and to impart some real knowledge of real estate. Now it was too late. The anger of the students that Trump and Michael Sexton cheated had now formed into a huge tsunami that was rolling, faster and higher, towards Trump's golden tower.

"Steve Miller," intoned Forge.

"Are you going to do this all day?" complained Trump.

"Same answer?"

"Same answer," replied Trump.

In fact, Steve Miller was a good guy. Late in the game, he had been brought in to check the backgrounds of the mentors. Like me, he was trying to run a straight-up operation. But it was all to no avail.

"Derek McNulty, Rick McNally."

"How many more do you have? How many more names do you have?" whined Trump. "Mr. Trump," replied Forge, "you're the one who wants to get through this quickly. Just answer the questions and we'll get through it quickly."

"You're not going to get anything through quickly," pouted Trump. "You don't want to get anything through quickly. Same answer."

Jerry Stanton, Johnny Burkins, Gerald Martin, Chris Lefrance, Steve Goff, James Webb. "Same answer to your harassment questions."

The names continued: Chris Lombardo, Keith Holley, Keith Sperry, Howard Bell, Howard Haller, Bob Serafine, Bob Steenson, Jerry Moore, Joe Labore, Mike McMenamy, Rick McNally, Mike Casper, Tim Gorsline, Geoff Nowlin, Steve Gilpin (*again* Forge asked Trump if he knew me!), James Christ, Alex Grist, Mike Weber, Don Sexton, Gary Stanton, Gary Sturgeon.

"Same answer." He said he didn't know. He claimed that it had been too many years. Forge decided to try a different approach. Perhaps Donald Trump, being the "genius" businessperson that he claimed to be, was better at remembering faces rather than names. Forge took out a sheet of photographs and put it on the table.

"Mr. Trump, let's get away from the names and see if you recognize any faces. I've placed in front of you a photo lineup, with three rows of eight photos per row, so that's a total of twenty- four photos. Do you recognize any of the people depicted on this exhibit?"

"What year was this picture taken?" asked Trump. "Different years."

"I think I should be entitled to know what year it was taken," insisted Trump. "When were they taken? How many years ago?"

"Different years."

"Well, I think you should find out. I mean—"

"Do you recognize any of the—" asked Forge.

"Are you allowed to find out when they were taken?"

"You know," Petrocelli told Trump, "you just have to answer the questions and get through this. These questions are what they are. If you're not able to recognize someone because he won't tell you when the pictures are taken, that's on him."

"Okay," said Trump.

"Do you recognize anyone whose photo is on here?"

"No. No, I don't."

Donald Trump's defense was this: since he was a billionaire with so many global business interests, he could not possibly remember every person who had ever worked for him. He didn't admit that he never "hand-picked" his speakers and mentors; it was just that their hiring had taken place so many years ago that he simply couldn't remember. And anyway, he had hired Michael Sexton to run the company, and Sexton was an outstanding guy, so what was the problem? Furthermore, Trump said that he was regularly provided with positive student reviews, proving to him that the students were satisfied, and that the company was running as it should. In fact, this wasn't the first time Donald Trump had sworn he didn't know me. Three years earlier, on September 12, 2012, during his deposition in the Makaeff case, this exchange had occurred: "How about Stephen Gilpin?" asked attorney Rachel Jensen. "Do you know who that is?" Trump replied, "I think these are names of people that I taught where—I think I know their names because I saw resumés, and I would see resumés of instructors, because it was important to me that we got good instructors. So I don't know if that's what you're referring to. But I've met numerous instructors, and I've also—this is over a period of years. And I've also seen the resumés of virtually everybody. So that's where they sound familiar to me; and in some cases, I know them better because I've met them."

"Sure," said Jensen. "Which instructors did you meet?"

"I believe [Columbia University professor] Donald Sexton and [Columbia University adjunct professor] Mr. [Jack] Kaplan. I believe perhaps [attorney and author John V. "J.J."] Childers.

I've met a number of them. I don't know their names. I mean, you're talking about years ago. This is actually years ago."

The men he named had written Trump's wealth-building books for him. They weren't Trump University live event instructors. He claimed not to know me or any other Trump University mentors or speakers. During the Cohen deposition, Forge asked Trump if he had ever personally visited a workshop. Trump spoke about two or three occasions when he was in Florida, and then talked about how on some weekends he would drop in unannounced to a Trump University workshop. He'd stand in the back of the room and observe, and he testified that the presentations were very professional and that he was satisfied with their quality. Conveniently, of course, the impromptu visits were not recorded on his calendar, he didn't tell anyone he was going, and despite being one of the most recognizable human beings on the planet, not one person saw him.

Actually, that's not quite true. He said, "For the most part I stood in the back of the room where they couldn't see me—a couple would turn around and saw me. And I think that they liked that they saw me there." Was Donald Trump actually saying under oath that he appeared at the back of the ballroom at a Trump University workshop, where at the front of the room his image was displayed on huge posters, as if he were a god, and he was recognized, and was not mobbed by adoring fans? That the Trump University team members by the doors didn't shriek with joy? That the speaker— who would have been an expert at "reading" the room—didn't spot him and say, "Hey, folks, guess what? The master himself is here! Donald Trump!"

If Donald Trump himself had appeared in the room, like a vision from heaven, every prospect in the place would have forked over thirty-five grand on the spot. But they didn't, because he was never there.

21.

On that warm December day, Donald Trump may have been feeling a little testy, because now he was facing not two but three major lawsuits over Trump University. On Saturday, August 24, 2013, the New York State Attorney General's office had filed a civil lawsuit accusing Trump University of engaging in illegal business practices.

The lawsuit, which sought restitution of at least $40 million, accused Trump, Sexton, and the Trump Organization of running the school as an unlicensed educational institution from 2005 to 2011, and making false claims about its classes in what was described as "an elaborate bait-and-switch."

Eric T. Schneiderman, the attorney general, charged that Trump appeared in advertisements for the school making "false promises" such as that Trump had "hand-picked" instructors to teach students "a systematic method for investing in real estate," when in fact Trump had not chosen even a single instructor at the school and had not created the curricula for any of its courses.

The suit also charged, "by ignoring the requirement that 'private career schools' be licensed by NYSED, Trump University also evaded an array of regulations and review by NYSED. For example, all school directors and teachers must be individually licensed by NYSED, all school sales agents working on commission must be individually certified by NYSED, and NYSED has authority to monitor schools' advertising to ensure it is not false, misleading, deceptive, or fraudulent, and is consistent with Article 22-A of the General Business Law. Each school must also pay NYSED tuition assessments based on its gross tuition income, in part to fund a 'tuition reimbursement account' for students who are owed refunds but are unable to obtain them from the school."

"No one, no matter how rich or famous they are, has a right to scam hardworking New Yorkers," said Schneiderman. "Anyone who does should expect to be held accountable." On Saturday evening, Michael "Pitbull" Cohen vigorously denied the accusations in the lawsuit, and said the school had received 11,000 student evaluations, in which 98 percent of the students said they were "extremely satisfied."

George Sorial, another lawyer for Trump (you may know his name from his occasional appearances on *The Apprentice*), called the lawsuit politically motivated. He said that Schneiderman had asked Trump and his family for campaign contributions and had become angry when denied.

"This is tantamount to extortion," claimed Sorial.

I received a subpoena from the New York attorney general, and knew my turn on the hot seat was coming. Avi Schick coached me intensively for weeks into the wee hours of the morning, brainwashing me thoroughly. I was under enormous pressure to say "I don't recall" to every question. Schick encouraged me to think that the case was frivolous and that the attorney general had a personal vendetta against Donald Trump and wanted to look like a hero.

I wish instead of using Trump's lawyers and testifying for Trump that I had hired my own lawyer and answered questions independently. It would have made the case totally different. Unfortunately, I was duped. They duped me by saying I had to use their attorney. They duped me by questioning me every night for two to three hours even when I was exhausted and couldn't stand it any more. They would give me coffee and push me to exhaustion so that I couldn't fight back. They duped me because they would respond to everything I said, with, "Well, that didn't really happen, though. You heard that through somebody else, secondhand," even though they knew that what I was saying was true.

They questioned me under duress, creating a stressful situation and then asking the same questions over and over again, feeding me answers until I started to doubt what reality was. I had to respond to every question with, "I don't recall," "I wasn't present," or "I don't know what you're referring to."

I started to actually believe that I didn't know anything for sure. I questioned everything that I knew to be right and accurate. I questioned everything and then I questioned my clients. Did that conversation really happen? I remembered speaking to that person, but maybe I didn't.

If I didn't know where the information came from, the lawyer said, "You've got to say that you don't recall. Or that there's no relevance." They made me repeat the phrases over and over again. It wasn't enough for me to say, "I understand. I got it." They made me say, "Where are the documents? What are you referring to? That doesn't pertain to you. I'd like to see them documented."

Of course, all this pressure was put on me because they didn't want me to say what I really wanted to say. Eventually, I was sufficiently convincing. Donald Trump's legal team said, "We'll have him do the deposition tomorrow."

It was eleven o'clock at night. I was in Schick's office. Schick asked me what I wanted to do. I replied that I'd like to go home and rest. He said, "No, why don't we get you something to eat first? I know a good steakhouse down the block. I'll take you there."

This was the first time they had offered me anything more than coffee and cookies. I agreed, and Schick and I and another attorney walked to the steakhouse. It was a first-class eatery where a dinner might set you back two hundred bucks. Schick said, "Go ahead, get whatever you want." So I ordered a steak dinner. No booze, though. Schick and the other lawyer didn't eat anything. They just sat there and looked at papers while I ate. It was strange—I felt as though I were a prisoner being granted a last meal before my execution.

The next morning, while wearing a navy blue pinstriped suit because I wanted to look sharp, I parked my car in the garage opposite the courthouse. Reporters congregated in front of the courthouse, but Schick wanted me to avoid being seen by them. As Schick instructed me, I walked to a coffeeshop that was across the street from the courthouse, where he met me. From there he led me through an underground passage into the courthouse. We emerged near the elevators. I was impressed that they had secret tunnels into the courthouse, so that people could avoid using the front door and being exposed to the press.

In a conference room in the district attorney's office, I gave my deposition. I sat with Schick and another attorney from Trump's office. The district attorney was not there, but across from me sat New York attorney general Eric Schneiderman and his staff. To the right of me sat the stenographer. To my left was Schick.

I was sworn in. The district attorney immediately began to berate me, making me feel like I was a fraudulent criminal who needed to be locked up in prison. Maybe the guy had taken the same interrogation class as Michael "Pitbull" Cohen. The stenographer was a pleasant woman. I felt bad for her. We exchanged glances and she smiled at me as her fingers flew across the keys.

Schick and I had a system of signs by which he would tell me to say some things and not say other things. With an eye signal or a hand signal he would indicate, "Don't answer this question." He had trained me to ask for a break if I was feeling cornered, and if he saw by my body language or my voice that I was getting rattled or feeling defensive he'd immediately ask for a break. During a break, we went down to the coffee machine. Due to a cold, I was drinking tea. He would remind me to remember how we had prepped, admonishing me to stay cool and to always fall back on saying "I do not recall." Then we'd go back up, where I'd face more questions.

In response to some of the questions, Schick would go off like a bulldog. He would say, "You can't ask him that question," or "He ain't answering that question." He was a very tough attorney. He is a former district attorney from the State of New York and knew all the tricks of the trade. The way that they questioned me was sneaky. They'd say, "Isn't it true that you wrote such-and-such or said such-and-such," but they wouldn't show me the document I'd supposedly written. And they'd show me a document and it wasn't one that I had written.

At one point the district attorney asked me, "Isn't it true that you knew a Mr. Kevin, and you had advised him in the real estate market, and he went *bankrupt?*" I keep in touch with many of my clients, who are honest people trying to make a decent living, and it seemed to me that what he was saying simply wasn't true. This made me upset, and Schick had to call for a break and get me calmed down. "They're going to try to trip you up and suggest things that are not true," he told me in the hallway. "Just stay cool and stay focused on how we prepped you.

Okay?"

I gave my deposition, but in my mind the prosecuting attorney never asked the right questions. He asked me about my financial situation, and about my credentials and licensing as a real estate mortgage broker, and about how many deals I had done, and if I had ever been bankrupt. Perhaps they had me confused with one of the motivational speakers who had no real estate experience, but the questions they asked seemed pointless. They accused me of things that I had never done, which also seemed pointless and was personally offensive. If the State of New York had wanted to effectively question me about the operation of Trump University and my personal experiences working for the organization, the district attorney should have asked me about the confused and angry students who called the hotline.

They should have asked about Sunil in Phoenix, Arizona, who could have gone to jail for following the instructions of his Trump University mentor. They should have asked me about the workshop speakers who filled the heads of their students with either Wikipedia rubbish or dangerous nonsense that would ruin their chances of success. They should have asked me about how I rushed from city to city, attending workshops and trying to "save clients," as Brad Schneider had put it so succinctly.

I would never perjure myself, but neither would I volunteer information that wasn't requested. Like many who are dominated and abused by a powerful authority, I was so committed to the team that I felt like I could not rebel against Trump University. I felt I had lost my sense of who I was and what I was doing. This was the opposite of feeling accepted. I felt owned. When it was all over, I felt that everything I said had been irrelevant.

Afterward, Avi Schick said to me, "Good job. They got nothing on you. You're done. You can put all of this behind you. Enjoy your life."

When I drove home, I found reporters camped out in front of my house. So I just kept driving. I was emotionally exhausted. I didn't want to be bothered. I didn't want to talk to anybody. I didn't take calls. I had no comment. I felt hurt that the media portrayed all the mentors as unqualified, because Trump University did have at least one white knight: me. But the prosecutors were also fundamentally right, of course. I knew that our mentors had not been chosen for their real estate knowledge.

A few weeks after I had left Trump University, I picked up a one-year consulting job at the Real Estate Education Center (REEDC) on West Thirty-Seventh Street. It's a NYSED- approved school, and they had heard about me being "the Trump kid" and they wanted me to run the bus tours and teach some courses.

After teaching at Real Estate Education Center for a few months, I received a phone call from a woman named Myrna at a school called New York Real Estate Institute (NYREI) located on West Thirty-Sixth Street, just around the block from REEDC.. She told me that her boss, Richard Levine, who was the head of the school, had heard about me and wanted to talk to me. She asked me to come to NYREI to talk with them. Five times I agreed and five times I called back to cancel because I was doing well and had a contract with REEDC.

On my fifth call, Levine got on the phone and said, "What is wrong with you? Why can't you walk over here and meet with me for five minutes?"

"Because I have no intention of working for you or your school," I replied. "But I'll give you five minutes." I went over there, and Levine and Myrna took me into an empty classroom. I sat down in my expensive three-piece-suit, as if this were a complete waste of time, which my demeanor reflected. I said to Levine, "Who the fuck are you and what do you want?"

After asking Myrna to leave the room he got up and sat on the corner of the desk with his hands crossed and said, "I'm Donald Trump's best friend and golf partner."

"Because you're working at REEDC," he continued, "I've lost over a million dollars in tuition money. You owe me."

"Okay, so you think I owe you." *Christ*, I thought. *There's no escaping the long arm of Donald Trump.*

Levine gave me a tight smile. "I would like to offer you the opportunity to run my school." I was dumbfounded.

"What?" I replied.

"I'm Donald Trump's friend," he repeated, stabbing the air with

his finger. "You went to work for the wrong school. You were supposed to come work for *me*." This man wasn't kidding. I could feel
myself being drawn back into the Trump tribe.

Levine then told me that based on consultation between Donald
Trump and Michael "Pitbull" Cohen—who unbeknownst to me was
Richard Levine's cousin and good friend—Cohen had told Levine
that I had done a good job at Trump University and that he would
be a "complete idiot" if he didn't hire me.

In a sense, NYREI was a reboot of Trump University. I saw it as
an opportunity to legitimize the courses and ideas that had been of
value at Trump University, and bring them into a legitimate education delivery system. I stated my terms, which included complete
control of the school. He accepted, and I was named director.

The February 2011 press release read in part, "We are proud to
welcome onboard our new director, Stephen Gilpin, a seasoned real
estate advisor and mentor from Trump Entrepreneur Initiative and
mentor to countless successful professionals. In Stephen's hands,
our new investor-targeted education initiative is already garnering
acclaim among students and professionals."

I served until August 2016. My departure was not a happy one,
because, like my tenure at Trump University, the company fell short
of its financial obligations towards me. History repeated itself, and
I finally learned my lesson about the Trump Organization and
anyone involved in it.

On Friday, January 20th, 2017 Donald Trump was inaugurated
as the 45th President of the United States of America. On March
31st, 2017 Judge Gonzalo P. Curiel approved a $25 million settlement
for the three cases against Trump University. *The New York Times*

reported that this would allow the members of the class action lawsuits to recoup up to 90 percent on the dollar for what they paid.

Judge Curiel said he thought the settlement was the best possible outcome. State Attorney General Eric Schneiderman said that he hoped the settlement would bring "relief—and hopefully much needed closure—to the victims of Donald Trump's fraudulent university."

As a condition of the settlement, Trump did not admit fault for the claims of fraud, and nor did he apologize. While the settlement was higher than anyone had anticipated, very few people anticipated that Donald Trump, the man who had cheated the people who had trusted him the most, would actually be elected president.

However, even after everything, I still believe that Trump University could have been a force for good. I'm passionate about educating people in the business of real estate. There's nothing more satisfying—or potentially profitable—than taking a run-down building, rehabbing it, adding value, and giving it a new life. But real estate investing is not a business for anyone who is inexperienced or who approaches it casually. It's incredibly hard work and you have to know what you're doing.

You also need the very best mentors. Donald Trump had been taught the business by his father, Fred Trump, a hugely successful developer. And who had taught Fred Trump? His mother, Elizabeth Christ Trump. Fred Trump built his career on the success of his mother and then passed his knowledge to his son. Both father and son benefitted from the wisdom and experience of their elders.

And now we see Eric, Don Jr., and Ivanka Trump being groomed for success the same way Fred Trump prepared his son Donald.

Good for them. There's nothing wrong with any of that. Knowledge and experience should be passed from generation to generation, and from mentor to student. I believe this at my core, and I try to do it every day with my colleagues.

Sadly, the students who paid thousands of dollars—in many cases their life savings—to Trump University did not receive the experience and wisdom of Donald Trump. They received the fantasies and platitudes of professional motivational speakers who knew nothing about real estate. What many of these hopeful students needed was not *motivation*—they had plenty of that—but real *information* and *guidance*. These could have been provided. Actually teaching our students would have been easy. They were eager to learn. At the end of the day, would all of them have been successful in real estate? No. It's a very tough business. Many of our students would not have succeeded no matter what we told them. But they all deserved their money's worth, and they all deserved a fair shot at the American dream.

EPILOGUE

After much controversy and a very ugly campaign, on November 9th, 2016, Donald J. Trump was elected 45th President of the United States. Throughout the campaign, I was fairly active on social media. I knew that the second trial, which included mostly West Coast and disgruntled students not named in the first suit, was coming up fast. I tried several times in the preceding months to contact "my attorney" to reiterate that I was not going to participate in this new trial. He never returned my calls or emails, so I quietly assumed I had escaped the potential rerun of the New York trial. I had said that if called, this time I would be a hostile witness.

The trial was quickly approaching, and still I had heard nothing. During the campaign, Trump had mentioned several times that he was going to reopen TEI once the situation was dealt with. I figured President Trump would now have to settle.

One day, as I was gathering research for this book, my cell phone rang. I answered hesitantly, as I did not recognize the California area code or number. "Hi Steve, this is Jill Martin. I'm calling about the upcoming trial regarding the Trump Entrepreneur Initiative."

That's what they were finally calling themselves. "We have been watching you on social media, so I am happy to inform you that we will not be needing you to testify this time." Was I hearing her correctly? A few days later, I received another call from Jill. She repeated what she had said a few days earlier. I asked her a lot of questions regarding the release of my obligations to Mr. Trump and the university.

At the end of the call, she suggested I "watch" what I write on social media. Watch what I write on social media? Where did that come from, and what did that mean? Last I checked, we had freedom of speech in this country. The man she worked for was certainly using it. Nonetheless, a bit intimidated by her comment, I quickly took down everything I had ever posted.

I wasn't feeling very confident after that conversation, so I put in a call to Mark Covais at Trump Initiative. I explained to him that Trump's attorney had just called to tell me that they would not be needing me to testify. He said he thought that since Trump had just been elected he would probably settle the suit. I asked about the terms of the settlement ($25 million) and whether I would be seeing any of that money. He apologized and told me, "not this time." We laughed. I told him not to worry that I might write a book someday. We talked about what I was doing since my tenure at NYREI had ended. We discussed how ironic it was that the person who worked for me at Trump University and then at NYREI had managed to cut me out of everything I had been doing there. Mark asked how you cut out the "brand." Good question. I often wonder that myself. Mark suggested that I apply to one of the 4,400 government jobs that Trump had to fill. Was that a back door way of telling me I could have a job in Trump's administration? I thought about that for all of two seconds. Uh, NO!

Some may question why I stayed so long, since I realized fairly early on what was happening there. The answer is simple. I just couldn't abandon those students, a number of whom spent their life savings to better their lives. They were suffering, and I needed to help as many as I could.

I continue to build business models as well as coach, mentor, and educate investors. My REO bus tours lead new as well as seasoned investors into distressed neighborhoods across the country. To me, distressed property sales are both altruistic and profitable endeavors. I believe that rebuilding neighborhoods only helps create stronger communities. This is the philosophy I took with me to Trump University, and it remains with me years later. I am happy to say that I am still coaching and mentoring many of the abandoned Trump University students. A lot of them have become friends as well as investment partners. I only regret the situation that brought us together.

You can always ask someone that knows me, "Where in the world is Steve Gilpin?" I can guarantee it will be some place different from the last time you asked.

REFERENCES

(in chronological order)

U.S. Patent and Trademark Office Trademark/Service Mark Application, Principal Register. Serial Number: 78462175, "Trump University. " Filing Date: 08/04/2004; registration date 07/04/2006.

Garland, Kevin. "Tuck professor aids 'Trump University'." *The Dartmouth* (Dartmouth, MA), June 1, 2005. http://www.thedartmouth.com/article/2005/06/tuck-professor-aids-trump-university.

Hindo, Bryan. "Trump University: You're Wired!" Bloomberg.com, May 23, 2005.

"Trump Mortgage." Trumpmortgage.com. Internet Archive Waybackmachine snapshot, May 22, 2006. https://web.archive.org/web/20060522190229/http://www.trumpmortgage.com/home/index.php.

"Interview with Paul Quintal." December 14, 2006. https://www.smallbusinessadvocate.com/small-business-interviews/paul-quintal-4357.

Fredrickson, Tom. "Undoing of Trump Mortgage." Crain's New York Business. August 05, 2007. http://www.crainsnewyork.com/article/20070805/REG/70804018/undoing-of-trump-mortgage.

"Trump University Intro." Filmed May 2005. YouTube video, 02:16. Posted December 5, 2008. https://www.youtube.com/watch?v=BvaaeHP9xtQ.

Boyd, Christopher. "Dynetech Affiliates Sued in Texas for Staging 'Misleading' Seminars." *Orlando Business Journal*, October 5, 2009. https://www.bizjournals.com/orlando/stories/2009/10/05/story5.html.

Burnett, Richard. "Florida did little or nothing with complaints about Dynetech." *Orlando Sentinel*, November 18, 2009. http://www.orlandosentinel.com/business/os-dynetech-florida-20091111-story.html.

"Robbins Geller Rudman & Dowd Files Consumer Class Action against Trump University." Robbins Geller Rudman & Dowd LLP, April 30, 2010. https://www.rgrdlaw.com/cases-trump_university.html.

"The Donald As The Dean?" The Smoking Gun. July 13, 2010. http://www.thesmokinggun.com/documents/crime/donald-dean.

Viser, Matt. "Donald Trump's Airline Went from Opulence in the Air to Crash Landing." The Boston Globe (Boston, MA), May 27, 2016. https://www.bostonglobe.com/news/politics/2016/05/27/donald-trump-airline-went-from-opulence-air-crash-landing/zEf1Er2Hok2dPTVVmZT6NP/story.html.

State of Utah, Plaintiff vs Cary K Beagley, Defendant. Securities Fraud document. August 29, 2011. http://www.securities.utah.gov/dockets/cr0048901.pdf.

"Letter: Donald Trump responds to Lazarus' Column." LA Times, December 13, 2007. http://www.latimes.com/business/la-fi-trumpreply16dec16-story.html.

Lazarus, David. "Trump spins in foreclosure game." LA Times, December 12, 2007. http://www.latimes.com/business/la-fi-lazarus12dec12-column.html

Osdol, Paul Van. "Pittsburgh woman says she's out $200,000 after attending Trump University." WTAE. May 16, 2016. http://www.wtae.com/article/pittsburgh-woman-says-she-s-out-200-000-after-attending-trump-university/7480129.

"Trump University 2010 Playbook." http://static.politico.com/25/88/783a0dca43a0a898f3973da0086f/trump-university-playbook.pdf.

"Donald Trump on President-Elect Obama: 'He Cannot Do Worse Than Bush'" (rush transcript of On the Record, November 5, 2008). Fox News, November 6, 2008. http://www.foxnews.com/story/2008/11/06/donald-trump-on-president-elect-obama-cannot-do-worse-than-bush.html.

"Denise DeVoe - NED Alliance - American Entrepreneur - Trump Institute Seminar "guru" a complete fraudster - scam seminar cost thousands - teaches nothing Nationwide." Ripoff Report. December 25, 2008. http://www.ripoffreport.com/reports/denise-devoe-ned-alliance-american-entrepreneur-trump-institute/nationwide/denise-devoe-ned-alliance-american-entrepreneur-trump-institute-seminar-guru-a-c-404867.

Cassidy, John. "What Sort of Man is Donald Trump?" The New Yorker, January 4, 2016. http://www.newyorker.com/news/john-cassidy/what-sort-of-man-is-donald-trump.

"Trump, His Fake University, and the (Former) Plaintiff." The Rude Pundit, May 05, 2016. http://rudepundit.blogspot.com/2016/05/trump-his-fake-university-and-former.html.

Request to Open Investigation into Trump University, LLC—Consumer Protection Division Houston Regional Office. October 7, 2009. https://assets. documentcloud.org/documents/2850971/Trump-U-Documents.pdf.

Feiden, Douglas. "Trump U. hit by complaints from those who paid up to 30G." *Daily News*, May 30, 2010. http://www.nydailynews.com/news/ trump-u-hit-complaints-paid-30g-return-article-1.446342.

Barbaro, Michael. "New York Attorney General is Investigating Trump's For-Profit School." *The New York Times*, May 19, 2011. http://www.nytimes. com/2011/05/20/nyregion/trumps-for-profit-school-said-to-be-under-investi- gation.html.

Appeal from the United States District Court for the Southern District of California. Makaeff v. Trump University. California Anti-SLAPP Statute/ Defamation. Filed April 17, 2013. Argued and Submitted January 18, 2012. http:// cdn.ca9.uscourts.gov/datastore/opinions/2013/04/17/11-55016.pdf.

Feuer, Alan. "Trump University Made False Claims, Lawsuit Says." *The New York Times*, August 23, 2013. http://www.nytimes.com/2013/08/25/nyregion/ trump-university-made-false-claims-lawsuit-says.html.

Depositions; Tarla Makaeff, et al., on Behalf of Themselves and All Others Similarly Situated vs Trump University LLC, et al., United States District Court Southern District of California. August 6, 2014. Case 3:10-cv-00940-GPC-WVG Document 339 Filed 07/25/14.

Matter of People of the State of N.Y. by Eric T. Schneiderman v Trump Entrepreneur Initiative LLC. Decided on March 1, 2016. http://law.justia.com/cases/new-york/ appellate-division-first-department/2016/451463-13-16094-16093.html.

Severns, Maggie. "Trump University: Teaching Real Estate—and Making Money." *Politico*, March 10, 2016. http://www.politico.com/story/2016/03/ trump-university-profits-220595.

Barbaro, Michael and Steve Eder. "At Trump University, Students Recall Pressure to Give Positive Reviews." *The New York Times*, March 11, 2016. https:// www.nytimes.com/2016/03/12/us/politics/donald-trump-trump-university. html.

United States District Court Southern District of California. Tarla Makaeff, Sonny Low, J.R. Everett and John Brown, on Behalf of Themselves and All Others Similarly Situated vs Trump University LLC. Order Regarding Motion to Withdraw. March 21, 2016. http://www.politico. com/f/?id=00000153-9f99-d022-ad57-ffddf4d80002.

Cohen vs. Donald J. Trump, Low et. al vs. Trump University, LLC., et al. "Important Documents." Filed 5/27/16. http://www.trumpuniversitylitigation. com/Home/Documents.

Stuart, Tessa. "Meet the Trump University Teacher at Center of Class-Action Suit." *Rolling Stone*, June 3, 2016. http://www.rollingstone.com/politics/news/meet-the-trump-university-teacher-at-center-of-class-action-suit-20160603.

Bennett, Dalton, Tom Hamburger, and Rosalind S. Helderman. "Donald Trump said 'University' was all about education. Actually, its goal was: 'Sell, sell, sell!'" *The Washington Post*, June 4, 2016. https://www.washingtonpost.com/politics/donald-trump-said-university-was-all-about-education-actually-its-goal-was-sell-sell-sell/2016/06/04/5b6545d0-2819-11e6-ae4a-3cdd5fe74204_story.html?utm_term=.04b6e0f89861.

"Former Texas Official says he was told to drop Trump University probe." CBS/AP, June 5, 2016. http://www.cbsnews.com/news/former-texas-official-says-he-was-told-to-drop-trump-university-probe/.

Griffin, Drew and Katie Lobosco. "Trump University's 'top' instructor was to sell, not teach." CNNMoney, July 13, 2016. http://money.cnn.com/2016/07/13/news/trump-university/index.html.

Bixenspan, David. "Debunking Donald Trump: The Ultimate 'Birther' Conspiracy Timeline." Law Newz, September 16, 2016. http://lawnewz.com/high-profile/donald-trump-barack-obama-birther-timeline-conspiracy/.

Wemple, Eric. "CNN Host totally owns Trump Lawyer Michael Cohen." *The Washington Post*, August 17, 2016. https://www.washingtonpost.com/blogs/erik-wemple/wp/2016/08/17/cnn-host-totally-owns-trump-lawyer-michael-cohen/?utm_term=.56ac0618cc97.

Horowitz, Jason. "For Donald Trump's Family, an Immigrant's Tale With 2 Beginnings." *The New York Times*, August 21, 2016. https://www.nytimes.com/2016/08/22/us/politics/for-donald-trumps-family-an-immigrants-tale-with-2-beginnings.html.